GRAND PRIX

First published in 1988 by
The Hamlyn Publishing Group Limited
a division of The Octopus Publishing Group
Michelin House, 81 Fulham Road, London SW3 6RB
and distributed for them by
Octopus Distribution Services Limited
Rushden, Northamptonshire NN10 9RZ

This edition published in 1988 by Peerage Books

© 1988 by The Hamlyn Publishing Group Limited

ISBN 185052 008 9
Printed in Spain

PICTURES

Front cover Nigel Mansell in the 1988 Williams-Judd FW12.

Back cover 1988 cars and drivers: top, Gerhard Berger's Ferrari F1/87.88C; centre left, Nelson Piquet in Lotus strip; centre right, Alain Prost in McLaren strip; bottom, Alessandro Nannini's Benetton-Ford B188.

Half-title Alain Prost (McLaren-TAG MP4/3) completing his record-breaking 28th F1 victory in the 1987 Portuguese GP.

Title spread Ayrton Senna (Lotus-Honda 99T) negotiates the right-hander in Casino Square in 1987's Monaco GP – first F1 victory for the new 'active' suspension.

This spread Nelson Piquet (Williams-Honda FW11B), 1987 world champion, taking his fourth second place in six races in the French GP.

Pages 6-7 Main picture: Nigel Mansell tests the 3.5-litre Judd-powered Williams FW11C at Jerez, Spain, in the spring of 1988. Inset: Frank Williams.

CONTENTS

INTRODUCTION

Motor racing has been a major part of my life for longer than I care to remember. I watched my first race at the age of 15 – I hitch-hiked to Silverstone from our home in Nottingham – and I suppose that I have been actively involved almost ever since.

At first I wanted to drive. I was captivated by the exploits of the great sporting heroes – of Jim Clark, Stirling Moss, Jackie Stewart and Jochen Rindt. Then, as I began to compete regularly, I realized that an enormous gulf divides the great talents from the also-rans. Although I had my days, I fell firmly into the category of also-rans. Instead, I became an entrant.

There have been bad times and good times, but I regret none of them. A turning-point in my life came when I formed a company with a young English designer named Patrick Head. A genius in his own field, Patrick is the man behind the success of the current Williams Grand Prix cars. Without him, none of our results would have been possible.

It is therefore with great pleasure that I introduce you to the latest edition of *Grand Prix*. This is a book of superb quality, covering not only the early years of our sport but also the most recent developments. I am biased, of course, but I particularly commend the freshly-written Part III. Not only does it capture the atmosphere and feel of some years that I will never forget but also it brings to life, with dazzling illustrations, the colour and splendour of Grand Prix racing, 1988-style. I am often asked why racing is so expensive, and how we raise our money – but I think part of the answer lies right here, in *Grand Prix*. There is no doubt in my mind that Grand Prix racing is the most exciting and adrenalin-pumping sport known to man. Transmit that sport to nearly 60 countries sixteen times a year and you have television exposure that is matched only by the Olympics and the World Cup. They happen every four years, however; our sport never seems to stop.

Read this book and enjoy it – and don't leave it on your coffee table. I did, and it vanished. It is not difficult to see why.

FRANK WILLIAMS

THE FIRST EIGHTY YEARS

1906 AND ALL THAT

The origins of grand-prix racing lie in the Gordon Bennett Cup, an international race sponsored by an expatriate American newspaper magnate, in which each country could enter three cars of native manufacture. The first of these races was in 1900 and the last in 1905. By this time the French had become disenchanted with the entry limit: as the first great centre of the motor industry, France by now had many firms building racers, notably Panhard, Renault, Peugeot,

Mors, Clément-Bayard, Darracq, De Diétrich, Gobron-Brillié, Richard-Brasier, and Turcat-Méry. They wanted an open, international race in which all marques could compete.

And so, for 1906, the Automobile Club de France (ACF) organised the first-ever Grand Prix (Great Prize). It killed the Gordon Bennett Cup stone dead. The race was over a 103.2km (63.9-mile) circuit of public roads east of Le Mans. It was run over two days, the cars doing six laps on each day – a total of 1238.4km (767.8 miles). The victor was Renault's chief test engineer, Ferenc Szisz, in a 13-litre, 90hp racer, averaging 101.2km/h (62.7 mph); second was the Italian Felice Nazzaro in a 16.3-litre, 100hp FIAT.

Preceding two pages *Some early Gordon Bennett races were run concurrently with major inter-city events. The last and most notorious of these was the 1903 Paris–Madrid race, which was stopped at Toulouse after several drivers and* spectators had been killed in accidents. The best-known fatality was Marcel Renault (one of the car-making brothers) seen at the wheel of his 6.5-litre light racer a few minutes before it overturned at Couhé-Verac, south of Poitiers.*

Left *Winner Léon Théry in a Richard-Brasier leads the Hon. C.S. Rolls in a Wolseley in the last of the Gordon Bennett Cup races, run on a twisty circuit in the Auvergne (France) in 1905. He averaged 77.9km/h (48.3mph).*

Above *Two of the 13-litre Renault racers in the pit lane during the 1906 Grand Prix, run on a circuit of closed public roads a few miles east of Le Mans. The race was held on two of the hottest days of the decade and many drivers suffered eye injuries from flying grit and molten tar. The winning driver, Ferenc Szisz, had been Louis Renault's riding mechanic in the 1903 Paris–Madrid race.*

Right *Szisz speeds in his 13-litre, 90bhp Renault through La Ferté-Bernard on his way to victory in the 1906 Grand Prix.*

Below *FIAT's Felice Nazzaro, who had come second in 1906, turned the tables on Szisz in the 1907 race near Dieppe. FIAT were pioneers in the use of overhead valves in racing cars.*

RACING TOWARDS THE WAR

Through 1907-8 the Grand Prix de l'ACF established itself as the world's premier motor race, and during the years of weight limitations (*see below*) engine capacities of 18 litres and more became commonplace. Racing techniques developed, pit procedures improved, and many national racing colours were adopted.

In 1907 the Grand Prix was run over a 76.9km (47.7-mile) circuit near Dieppe, and this time Nazzaro's 4-cylinder, 16.3-litre FIAT, developing 130bhp, beat Szisz's 13-litre Renault by over six minutes. Worse (in French eyes) was to follow at Dieppe the following year, when Christian Laütenschlager, foreman-tester at Mercedes' factory, won in a 12.8-litre racer designed by Paul Daimler – and, moreover, German Benz cars came second and third.

Owing to a depression in the car industry, the next true Grand Prix did not take place until 1912, when it was again held at Dieppe. It was run concurrently with a race for *voiturettes* (3-litres maximum) sponsored by *L'Auto* magazine. The race was a triumph for a new French hero, Georges Boillot, driving the revolutionary new Peugeot L76 with its twin-overhead-camshaft, four-valves-per-cylinder engine of only 7.6 litres. Boillot won again at Amiens the following year.

Rules and Regulations: 1906-14

The ACF chopped and changed the regulations for its Grand Prix, taking account of developments in car and engine design. The main provisions for the six Grands Prix during this period were as follows:

1906 Weight limit of 1000kg (2200lb).
1907 Maximum fuel consumption permitted: 30 litres/100km (6.6gal/62 miles), equivalent to about 9½ miles per gallon.
1908 Combined area of piston heads: 75cm^2 (117 sq in), equivalent to a bore diameter of 155mm (6in) for 4-cylinder and 127mm (5in) for 6-cylinder engines.
1909–11 Grand Prix in abeyance owing to recession in French car industry.
1912 No weight or engine-capacity restrictions.
1913 Maximum fuel consumption permitted: 20 litres/100km (4.4gal/62 miles), equivalent to about 14 miles per gallon. Weight restricted to between 800 and 1100kg (1760 and 2420lb).
1914 Engine capacity 4½ litres maximum; weight 1100kg (2420lb) maximum.

Felice Nazzaro (1881–1940)

Nazzaro, the greatest Italian driver of the period up to World War I, was apprenticed to the FIAT company at an early age, and was for some time employed as a chauffeur by Vincenzo Florio. He became a test engineer and then a racing driver for FIAT in the first years of this century, the company's formidable trio of drivers being made up by Vincenzo Lancia and Alessandro Cagno.

Nazzaro sprang to prominence in 1905 when he and Cagno took second and third places in the Gordon Bennett Cup in massive 75bhp FIATs; the following year he came second to Szisz in the first-ever Grand Prix. Nazzaro's greatest year, however, was 1907, when he won the three premier races of the season in three FIATs of quite different specification: the Targa Florio in the 7.4-litre 28-40hp '20-B' model; the Kaiserpreis (the German equivalent of a Grand Prix) in the 8-litre Taunus model; and the French Grand Prix with an F2, a massive 16.3-litre racer capable of 177km/h (110mph). His crowning achievement after World War I came in 1922 when, at the age of 41, he won the French Grand Prix at Strasbourg in a 2-litre Fiat Tipo 804. These cars were remarkably fast for their day and capacity, but efforts to reduce their weight had made them dangerously fragile. (Nazzaro's pleasure in his outstanding victory was soured by the death in this race of his nephew Biaggio, in a similar Fiat, who was thrown onto the track when his 804's rear axle snapped.) He retired from racing after his car broke down in the Italian Grand Prix of 1924, but he remained on Fiat's staff until shortly before his death in 1940.

Above *Poster for the 1912 Grand Prix — the first for four years — and the Coupe de L'Auto voiturette race run at the same meeting.*

Right *1912 Grand Prix: Georges Boillot on his way to victory in the advanced Peugeot L76. The race was run over two days, Boillot brilliantly nursing his car home after it lost two of its four gears on the second day. The Peugeot's triumph signalled the end of the slow-revving, mammoth-engined racers in grands prix.*

Georges Boillot (1885–1916)

During the Coupe de *L'Auto* of 1913, Georges Boillot was in the lead when, to the surprise of the Peugeot mechanics, he pulled into the pits, climbed out of his car and called for a glass of wine. Having unhurriedly quenched his thirst, he enquired casually as to how his rivals were doing, climbed back into his car, and drove to victory. The episode was characteristic of a man whose histrionic temperament, vanity and brilliance as a driver lent excitement to racing in the last few years before World War I and made him the idol of the French public.

Boillot made his name as a development engineer and driver of the bizarre Lion-Peugeot V-twin *voiturettes*. He and his team-mates Jules Goux (as good a driver as Boillot, though less flashy), and Paul Zuccarelli (formerly an engineer with Hispano-Suiza) all helped the brilliant Swiss engineer Ernest Henri in the design of the innovative Peugeot L76 and its successor developed for the 1914 Grand Prix (*see overleaf*).

At the outbreak of war he joined the French air force – one of the first pilots in a unit known as *Les Sportifs*. He died in May 1916 when, in a spirit typical of his performance on the racetrack, he took on seven German scouts singlehanded: the odds were hopeless and he was shot out of the sky.

Above Boillot also won the 1913 Grand Prix, which had reverted to a single-day event. His team-mate Jules Goux took another L76 to victory in the famous Indianapolis 500 that year, and they later joined forces to break a world record by covering more than 171km (106 miles) in one hour.

Left Boillot first gained fame driving in voiturette *races*. Here he is on his way to winning the 1913 Coupe de L'Auto at Boulogne in a 3-litre Peugeot.

THE 1914 GRAND PRIX

The French were vehemently chauvinistic in their attitude toward the Grand Prix: they regarded it as their race, and hated to see victory going to foreign cars. It is easy to imagine the emotional frenzy of the crowd at the 1914 Grand Prix (at Lyon), which was run only four weeks before the outbreak of World War I. It was, in fact, one of the most significant grands prix in history. Technically it proved to be a contest between what were then the two most advanced marques in the world – Peugeot of France and Mercedes of Germany. The 4.5-litre Peugeot engine, designed by Ernest Henri, can be regarded as the ancestor

of the modern high-performance car engine: it used twin overhead camshafts to operate four valves per cylinder, and developed 112bhp at the then high speed of 2,900rpm. To improve cornering performance the Peugeots were fitted with brakes on all four wheels (the first time the system was used in the Grand Prix). Henri's opposite number in the Mercedes camp was Paul Daimler (son of the car pioneer). His cars also had engines of 4.5 litres (the maximum capacity permitted for this race), with single overhead camshafts, and four valves and three sparking plugs per cylinder; they developed 115bhp at 3,200rpm. Both cars used shaft drive rather than chains, developed power at more usable engine speeds than the vast, slow-revving cars of earlier days, and had far better handling.

The German team consisted of old hands

Right Louis Wagner in his second-placed Mercedes on the back stretch of the 1914 Grand Prix circuit at Givors, south of Lyon. Though advanced in engine specification, the German cars had no front-wheel brakes, the foot-pedal operating a drum on the drive shaft while the outside hand-brake acted only on the rear wheels.

Left *The winner, Christian Laütenschlager, on the steep, winding hill that culminated in the Piège de la Mort (Deathtrap) hairpin bend. He averaged 105.7km/h (65.7mph) for the race.*

Below *Boillot in his Peugeot. Its long tail, fitted specially for the race, increased the car's top speed.*

such as Laütenschlager, Otto Salzer and ex-Fiat driver Louis Wagner, and newcomer Max Sailer. Peugeot were led by Boillot and Jules Goux.

In spite of a legend to the contrary, the Germans had not planned a detailed race strategy; but Sailer's impetuosity served his team well. He went off like a rocket and was 1½ minutes ahead of Boillot by the end of the third lap of the 37.5km (23.3-mile) circuit; on the fourth lap he broke the circuit record — and then one of his connecting rods snapped. He was out of the race, but his job was done: Boillot had already over-stretched his car in a rash attempt to keep pace with Sailer. By now Laütenschlager in the second Mercedes was beginning to press Boillot, who immediately stepped up his speed. But the Mercedes challenge was remorseless: by lap 17 (with only three to go) Laüenschlager had cut Boillot's lead to 14 seconds, and on the 18th he passed him. By now the Peugeot was sick and on the next lap it threw a valve. And so it was that Laütenschlager, Wagner and Salzer recorded the first-ever 1–2–3 Grand Prix victory, Goux's Peugeot limping in in fourth place. The vast French crowd was stunned — and the official band found itself unable to play the German national anthem because it had 'mislaid' the music.

Right The 1921 Grand Prix was run over the public-road circuit south of Le Mans that is now used for the 24-hour sportscar race. The picture shows the eight-cylinder Ballot driven by Louis Wagner (one of the Mercedes team in the 1914 race) into seventh place. The surface of the Le Mans circuit broke up during the race, which was described by one of the drivers of the winning Duesenberg team as 'a damn rock-hewing contest'.

THE 1920s

The ACF held the first post-war Grand Prix in 1921 on a new public-road course, 17.26km (10.7 miles) long, at Le Mans – essentially the circuit still used today for the famous Le Mans 24-hour race. The Club adopted the 3-litre Indianapolis race formula – and the race appropriately went to the American Jimmy Murphy in his straight-eight Duesenberg.

In 1922 Italy held its own grand prix at newly opened Monza. Fiat straight-six Tipo 804s won not only this race but the French Grand Prix at Strasbourg. Sunbeam built virtually a replica of the Fiat and won the 1923 French GP at Tours and the Spanish Grand Prix at San Sebastian.

The finest racers of the later 1920s were built by Alfa Romeo, Bugatti and Delage. Sunbeam had 'borrowed' Fiat engineers to build their winning racer. Alfa Romeo sent Enzo Ferrari to lure the greatest Italian designer of all away from Fiat:

Vittorio Jano, who produced the famous straight-eight P2, a quicker version of Fiat's superb 805. The P2, in the hands of Giuseppe Campari, won its first-ever grand prix (the French, at Lyon) in 1924, following it with the Italian and European (at Spa, Belgium), both going to Antonio Ascari.

Bugatti's most famous racer was the beautiful straight-eight Type 35 in its various forms, notably the 35C (1990cc, supercharged) and the 35B (2261cc, blown and unblown), both of these competing in the many free-formula races; there was also the Type 39 variant (1492cc, blown) to compete in the 1926-7 1½-litre GP formula.

But the dominant racer in the 1½-litre formula was the Delage. For 1926 the marque followed its fascinating, hugely complex 2-litre V12 racer with a superb 1½-litre straight-eight, the most innovative engine of its day, which in blown form developed a remarkable 170bhp. Its performance was initially hampered by heating problems, but for one glorious season (1927) ace driver Robert Benoist made mincemeat of the opposition. Then, for 1928, the *formula libre* (unlimited engine-capacity) was introduced.

Below Ettore Bugatti's masterpiece, the Type 35, first raced in the French Grand Prix of 1924. More than 200 in various forms were built over the next seven years. The Type 35B with supercharger was introduced in 1927; the beautifully maintained example shown here still competes regularly in Vintage races and is capable of more than 205km/h (130mph).

Left *Vittorio Jano stands in front of his first car for Alfa Romeo, the P2 grand-prix racer closely modelled on the Fiat 805 that he had helped to design. The P2 had three major triumphs in 1924.*

Below *Jano's greatest grand-prix car, the Alfa Romeo Tipo B (or P3), won practically everything in sight in seasons 1932-3. Light in weight, supremely agile, and handsome in appearance, the Tipo B's further development ceased with Alfa Romeo's near bankruptcy at the end of 1932.*

Rules and Regulations: 1921–33

1921 Minimum weight 800kg (1760lb); engine capacity 3 litres maximum.
1922–4 Minimum weight 650kg (1430lb); engine capacity 2 litres maximum.
1925 As above; riding mechanics banned but two-seat body still required; rear-view mirrors obligatory.
1926 Minimum weight 600kg (1320lb); engine capacity 1½ litres maximum; single-seat body style allowed.
1927 Minimum weight 700kg (1540lb); engine capacity 1½ litres maximum.
1928 Engine capacity: no limit; minimum weight 550–750kg (1210–1650lb), depending on engine size; race distance 600km (372 miles) minimum.
1929 Commercial petrol mandatory, with consumption limit of about 14.5 miles per gallon.
1930 As above, with option of adding 30 per cent benzole to commercial fuel.
1931 *Formula libre* (free formula); race duration 10 hours minimum.
1932 *Formula libre*; race duration 5–10 hours.
1933 *Formula libre*; race distance 500km (310 miles) minimum.

FREE FORMULA

The *formula libre*, which in various guises was to last until the end of the 1933 season, saw the departure of the Delage, Sunbeam and bankrupt Talbot from the grand-prix scene. At the end of the decade a new Italian marque, Maserati, made an impressive entrance, and in 1930 its powerful 2½-litre supercharged straight-eight gained five grand-prix victories. Ettore Bugatti responded with the twin-cam Type 51, powered by a supercharged straight-eight engine of 2 or 2.3 litres based on an American Miller design, and followed this with the powerful but tricky 4.9-litre Type 54.

Then, in 1932, came one of the most revered of all grand-prix racers: Vittorio Jano's masterpiece, the Alfa Romeo Tipo B, commonly known as the P3 – the first purpose-built *monoposto* (single-seat) GP car. The P3's supercharged straight-eight engine was originally of 2654cc and developed 215bhp. In the 1932 season it won all but two of the races it entered; in many events the Alfa works team, run by the young Enzo Ferrari, filled second and third spots as well. More powerful versions were developed over the next three seasons. And in the 1935 German Grand Prix the car achieved its apotheosis: a 3.8-litre version, driven with unparalleled brilliance by Tazio Nuvolari on a rain-soaked Nürburgring, humbled all nine of the supposedly unbeatable Mercedes-Benz and Auto Union racers developing at least 100bhp more than the Alfa.

Tazio Nuvolari (1892–1953)

'The Flying Mantuan' is still regarded by many as the greatest racing driver of all. At the height of his fame in the 1930s he was known simply but unequivocally as Il Maestro (The Master), and in Italy he was a national hero. On the racetrack his short, slight figure, clothed in a yellow turtle-neck sweater, sky-blue trousers, and brown shoes with yellow laces, was instantly recognisable. At the wheel, his extraordinary facial contortions belied the cool, unspectacular economy of his driving style. He was probably the inventor of the technique of fast cornering known as the four-wheel drift.

For most of the 1930s Nuvolari drove Alfa Romeos (and sometimes Maseratis), which from 1934 onwards were outclassed in specification and performance by the new Mercedes-Benz and Auto Union racers. An idea of Nuvolari's genius can be seen in the fact that in 1934–6 he won 14 grands prix and was placed in nine others, while the great Rudolf Caracciola, the number one driver of the Mercedes-Benz team, won nine and was placed in four. If his most famous victory was in the 1935 German Grand Prix an almost equally startling demonstration of his skill came in the 1934 Monza Grand Prix. In order to lighten his Maserati for the weigh-in before the race, his crew drained the hydraulic fluid from the brake system – and then forgot to put it back! In spite of having virtually no brakes, Nuvolari came in fifth.

His courage was legendary. In 1934, with his right leg encased in plaster seven weeks after he had broken it in a crash at Alessandria, he entered for the Avus Grand Prix on the circuit near Berlin. Although he had only one usable foot to actuate the accelerator, clutch, and brake pedals, he took fourth place. He broke ribs so often that he had a special 'corset' of bandages made for him so that he could race while the fractures were mending.

Nuvolari was strenuously wooed by the managers of the Mercedes and Auto Union teams, and eventually he joined Auto Union in 1938, finishing fourth in his first race and winning the Italian and Donington grands prix that season.

His career in major sports-car races was concentrated mainly in the years 1930–5. During that period he won the Mille Miglia twice (1930, 1933) and was second once (1934); he won the Targa Florio twice (1931, 1932), the Le Mans 24-hours once (1933), and the RAC Tourist Trophy race twice (1930, 1933).

Above *Tazio Nuvolari in his 1930s heyday. He was a motor-cycling champion before he became the greatest grand-prix and sportscar driver of the years before World War II.*

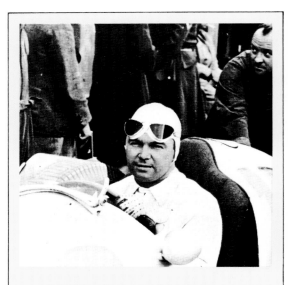

Rudolf Caracciola (1901–59)

In spite of his dark hair and Italian-sounding surname, Rudolf Caracciola was a German born in the Rhineland, the son of a hotelier of Remagen. He worked during the early 1920s for the Fafnir motor factory and drove the firm's 1.9-litre Type 471 sports car in his first race, at the Avus circuit, in 1922. His talent was soon spotted by Mercedes and he began his long career with the great Stuttgart firm in 1924, at first taking part mainly in hill-climb and sprint races. He was entered in the first-ever German Grand Prix, at the Avus in 1926, and leapt into immediate international prominence by winning the race, driving the ill-handling 2-litre Mercedes brilliantly on the rain-soaked track. Caracciola's skill in the wet was unrivalled in his day – he was known as Regenmeister (Rainmaster) and was unmatched in grand-prix racing until Stirling Moss reached his peak in the 1950s.

Caracciola proved himself one of the great grand-prix drivers in the 1935–9 seasons. There is no doubt that the Mercedes-Benz and, to a lesser extent, the Auto Unions of that period were greatly in advance of anything the Italians or the French manufacturers could put against them. But equally the cars needed drivers of outstanding skill to get the best out of them. Caracciola proved unquestionably the greatest of the team of Mercedes drivers of that era, winning 14 grands prix (including the German race five times) in the last six seasons before World War II.

Like other Mercedes and Auto Union drivers, Caracciola also competed in major hill-climb events in the 1930s. Although not so great in this field as 'Bergmeister' Hans Stuck, he broke the record for the notorious Klausen hill-climb in 1934 in a Mercedes W25.

GERMANY TRIUMPHANT

In 1933 the Nazi government in Germany began to subsidize the development of not one but two world-beating grand-prix teams: the well-established Mercedes-Benz stable and the newly emergent Auto Union, which was to build racers designed by Dr Ferdinand Porsche. That year the Association Internationale des Automobile Clubs Reconnus (AIACR), the grand-prix ruling body, announced that for 1934 the new formula would have a *maximum* weight limit of 750kg (1650lb), excluding fuel, oil, water and tyres.

For Mercedes, designer Hans Nibel's team produced the W25, powered by an advanced twin-cam straight-eight of 3360cc and with all-independent suspension. Porsche came up with

his sensational mid-engined V16 racer, with limited-slip differential but somewhat tail-happy handling. In 1935–7 both marques steadily developed and improved their racers (the Mercedes culminating in the awesome W125, which was getting 646bhp from its 5.66-litre engine). For 1938–9 the formula was changed to a *minimum* weight of 800kg (1760lb) and a maximum engine capacity of 3 litres supercharged and 4½ litres unsupercharged. The superb Mercedes W154 and its 1939 refinement, the W163 – a true masterpiece of engineering, its four-cam V12 engine producing 484bhp with two-stage supercharging – were matched by the equally powerful Auto Union D-Type.

From 1935 until the outbreak of World War II the German teams were not merely dominant but, collectively, virtually invincible. Allied to the astonishing power, sophistication and increasing reliability of their cars was the ruthlessly efficient organization of their works teams, and the Mercedes team manager, the rotund Alfred Neubauer, with his battered trilby and necklace of stopwatches, became an ominously familiar figure to rival teams all over Europe.

Alfa Romeo gave up the grand-prix battle, concentrating on *voiturette* racing and on the sports-car events they came to dominate with a series of brilliant Jano-designed cars. In 1938 Delahaye and Talbot briefly entered the lists with sadly inferior 4½-litre unblown racers. Maserati, with their handsome, very fast but unreliable 8CTF 3-litre supercharged racer produced on a shoestring, occasionally gave the Germans a scare (but the car's only real success came when it went to America and won the Indianapolis 500 race two years running). The period closed in September 1939 when Nuvolari, lured to Auto Union the year before, won the Yugoslav Grand Prix on the day war was declared.

Above *Caracciola in the Mercedes-Benz W154, in which he won the drivers' championship for the third year running in 1938. The V12 car was developed for the 3-litre formula introduced that year, and won six major races in five countries. Like the rival Auto Union D-type it used limited-slip differential, a refinement available on popular road cars only in the 1980s.*

THE WORLD CHAMPIONSHIPS

For 1948 the sport's new governing body, the Fédération Internationale de l'Automobile (FIA), specified a grand-prix formula (1½ litres blown, 4½ litres unblown) to suit existing (essentially pre-war) machinery. Best of the unblown cars were the Lago-Talbots; but the year belonged to the supercharged Alfa Romeo Tipo 158 Alfetta, which had been designed by Jano's chief aide, Gioacchino Colombo, in 1938. Alfa withdrew from racing in 1949 following the deaths of their three leading drivers — Jean-Pierre Wimille and the great veteran Achille Varzi in crashes and Count Carlo Trossi from cancer — and the season was dominated by a new *équipe*, Ferrari, and its rising star Alberto Ascari.

In 1950 the FIA launched two World Championships — one for constructors, the other for drivers. The formula was unchanged and the improved Alfetta, Tipo 159, triumphed in the first two years, Dr 'Nino' Farina taking the drivers' title in 1950 and Juan Manuel Fangio in 1951. Alfa Romeo then retired from racing.

For 1952–3 the FIA changed the specification to Formula B (or Formula 2 as it came to be called) — a *voiturette* class for unblown 2-litre cars. Ferrari was totally in charge in these two seasons, its four-cylinder Tipo 500 F2s winning 14 consecutive GPs.

Left *The Alfa Romeo Tipo 158, designed by Gioacchino Colombo (who later found fame with Ferrari), was originally intended for* voiturette *racing. The car dominated the grand-prix scene in 1948, was withdrawn in 1949, then won the new world championship in 1950 and 1951. Of its total of 33 grand-prix victories, 26 came in succession. By 1951 its final form (Tipo 159) was getting an astonishing 420bhp from its 1½-litre engine and could manage barely 2mpg on its alcohol fuel. The picture shows a Tipo 158 on the starting line at the famous Monza circuit.*

Right A view into the engine compartment of the Ferrari 500 F2 which Alberto Ascari drove to victory in the 1953 British Grand Prix. Relatively small and simple by Ferrari standards, the four-cylinder unsuper-charged engine developed 180bhp at 7,500rpm; its two twin-choke Weber carburettors are in the foreground. The 500 F2 won 30 out of its 33 races in two years.

Alberto Ascari (1918–55)

'Ciccio' Ascari, son of the great Alfa driver of the early 1920s, gained early racing experience on motorcycles, and had his first big motorcar race in 1940, when Enzo Ferrari offered him a drive in his first model, the Fiat-based Vettura 815, in the Mille Miglia. After the war he drove Cisitalias and works Maseratis for a few seasons. In 1949 Ascari and his mentor, Luigi Villoresi, joined Ferrari, Ascari winning the Italian and Swiss grands prix in Tipo 166s. Ascari's two greatest seasons were 1952 and 1953. The formula (2-litre, unsupercharged) was unexciting, but Ferrari's new chief designer, Aurelio Lampredi had come up with a car perfectly suited to its job, the Tipo 500 F2. Of the 14 consecutive grands prix won by Ferrari in those two seasons, Ascari took 11 and in both years ran away with the drivers' title by huge margins.

In 1954 Ascari was lured away to Lancia, then preparing its Jano-designed D50 V8s for the new 2½-litre formula. The following season the cars finally got onto the circuits, proving immensely fast, though difficult to handle. In the Monaco Grand Prix Ascari, leading on the 80th lap, came out of the tunnel, braked to negotiate the water-front chicane, locked one of his front wheels – and the car plunged into the harbour. Amazingly, Ascari escaped with bruises. Four days later he took a Ferrari sportscar to Monza to test his nerve. On his third lap the car struck the edge of the track and rolled over, Ascari dying soon afterwards. Like his father, he was killed at the age of 36 on the 26th day of the month.

Juan Manuel Fangio (born 1911)

Stirling Moss, number two to Fangio in the Mercedes team in 1955, regarded 'El Chueco' (Bandylegs) as the greatest grand-prix driver he had ever seen. Post-war, certainly, his record is incomparable: although Jim Clark, Jackie Stewart and Alain Prost all won more grands prix, none of them approached his astonishing wins-to-races ratio of 24 victories in 51 starts — all achieved, moreover, in a championship career that did not begin until he was 38 years old!

He learnt his trade in his native Argentina in the 1930s, driving in long-distance road races. His first experience in true racing cars was in 1948 when, after demonstrating his talent in a series of events in Buenos Aires, he was brought to Europe by Jean-Pierre Wimille to race Simcas. He won his first race (the San Remo Grand Prix). He was invited to join the Alfa Romeo works team for 1950, when he won three GPs and was runner-up in the championship; the following year he took the title.

His second and third titles came in 1954 and 1955 with Mercedes; the following year, the Germans having withdrawn from racing, he moved to Ferrari and took his fourth title. His fifth (and fourth in a row) was with Maserati. He retired in 1958.

Fangio's success was based on immaculate technique, a fine tactical sense, patience, and an unmatched ability to nurse ailing cars to victory. That he could also drive with unparalleled ferocity he showed in the title-clinching German Grand Prix of 1957, when he broke the lap record five times in the first 11 laps in his ageing Maserati 250F; lost over a minute in a disastrous refuelling stop; and finally destroyed the challenges of Hawthorn and Collins in the very fast Lancia-Ferraris on the 20th lap, when he sliced a further six seconds off an already astonishing lap record.

THE MERCS RETURN

For 1954 the FIA specified a 750cc blown/2½ litres unblown formula. Ferrari, Maserati and newcomers Lancia were joined, halfway through the season, by Mercedes-Benz, re-entering the grand-prix circus after 15 years; all of these marques opted for unblown engines. The German fuel-injected, straight-eight W196 racers, with novel space-frame chassis and aerodynamic bodywork, won the first GP they contested (the French at Reims) and dominated the rest of the season. Juan Manuel Fangio took the drivers' title, after starting the season with Maserati but then accepting a lucrative Mercedes offer. In 1955 the W196 was virtually unbeatable and Fangio took his third title. But Mercedes withdrew from all racing at the end of that season after one of their sportsracing 300SLR cars, 3-litre derivatives of the grand-prix car, had crashed at Le Mans, killing 89 people.

Left *Stirling Moss (6) and Juan Manuel Fangio (2) head the field in their Mercedes W196s in the 1955 Monaco Grand Prix; neither finished the race. The W196 was available with two variations of bodywork; the other had an all-enveloping streamlined body that gave it a higher top speed but was hard to manoeuvre accurately on twisty circuits.*

Right Alfred
Neubauer was team
manager of the
victorious Mercedes
grand-prix teams both
in the 1930s and in
the 1954–5 seasons.

Below Stirling Moss
aboard one of his
favourite cars, the
Maserati 250F, on his
way to victory in the
1956 Monaco Grand
Prix, which he led
from start to finish.
The 250F, partly
designed by Colombo,
was one of those cars
in which the whole is
much better than its
fairly conventional
parts might suggest.
In four seasons,
1954–7, it won 22
Formula 1 races, in-
cluding seven in 1957
when it took Fangio to
his fifth and final
drivers' title.

BRITISH BREAKTHROUGH

The last grand prix of the 1955 season, at Syracuse (Sicily), saw the Maserati team humbled by Tony Brooks' Connaught – the first all-British victory in a European GP since Henry Segrave's Sunbeam had won at San Sebastian in 1924.

The British were encouraged. And in 1956, while Fangio won his fourth title (in the very fast Jano-designed Lancia D50 V8, racing in Ferrari colours after the Lancia family sold their car interests to an industrial consortium), the aerodynamically advanced, 2½-litre, 4-cylinder Vanwall became competitive.

The following year, although thwarted again by Fangio winning his fifth and last title (with Maserati), Vanwalls in the hands of Stirling Moss, Brooks and Stuart Lewis-Evans began taking the chequered flag. In 1958 the British team fought a furious, season-long battle with the Ferrari Dino 246s driven by Mike Hawthorn and Peter Collins. Going into the final race, at Casablanca, the drivers' title lay between Moss and Hawthorn. By coming second Hawthorn clinched the title by a single point; but winner Moss had the satisfaction of securing the first-ever British constructors' title for Vanwall.

Left *Stirling Moss, with cups and victor's laurels after winning the 1957 Italian Grand Prix for Vanwall.*

Stirling Moss (born 1929)

Moss never won the drivers' title – he was runner-up four years running (1955–8) – but he was the greatest all-rounder since Nuvolari, excelling equally as a grand-prix, sportscar and rally driver. His first qualifying GP was the Swiss at Berne in 1951. In 1954 he bought a Maserati 250F, took third place in his first race, and was invited to join Maserati's works team. In that year's Italian GP at Monza he outdrove the W196s of Fangio and Hermann Lang until, with only 10 laps to go, his fuel tank sprang a leak. But this drive was enough to secure him a place in the Mercedes team for 1955, when he won the British GP. With Mercedes' withdrawal from racing, Moss rejoined Maserati for 1956 and won the Monaco and Italian GPs as well as many non-qualifying events. For 1957–8 he spearheaded Vanwall's campaigns, and also achieved one of his greatest victories, in the Argentine GP, in a prototype mid-engined Cooper.

For 1960 Moss drove the fast but fragile new Lotus 18, winning at Monaco but then suffering two broken legs when his car lost a rear wheel in practice for the Belgian GP – but he went on to win the U.S. GP later in the season. For 1961, still with the now outdated Lotus 18, he won the Monaco and German GPs against all odds. His racing career ended in 1962 when he suffered serious head injuries when crashing, inexplicably, in a race at the Goodwood Easter meeting.

THE MID-ENGINE TAKEOVER

The year 1958 was the end of the line for the classic front-engined grand-prix car. At their Surbiton (Surrey) garage the Cooper car company had launched a Formula 2 version of their hugely successful mid-engined, all-independently-sprung F3 racer. The new car, using a 1½-litre Coventry Climax engine descended from a fire pump, proved competitive. In January 1958, with a 2-litre Climax engine, the car was entered for the Argentine GP. The organisers at first thought the car was a toy – but Stirling Moss drove the Cooper to a stunning victory, at record speed, over the Ferrari and Maserati teams.

For 1959 a full 2½-litre Climax engine was ready and the Coopers put the other works teams to the sword, winning five GPs, taking the constructors' championship and giving Jack Brabham his first drivers' title. The following year – with BRM, Lotus and even Ferrari also fielding mid-engined cars – Cooper and Brabham took their titles even more decisively, winning six of the qualifying races.

Amid controversy (and bitterness among British interests) a 1½-litre formula had been declared for 1961. Ferrari had a potent mid-engined version of the V6 Dino 246, and it proved superior to the old F2 designs to which the shoe-string Cooper outfit was obliged to revert. The Dino 156 F1, as the new model was designated, was instantly recognizable by its two air-intake nostrils at the front; it gave Ferrari the constructors' title and American Phil Hill the drivers', after his closest challenger, team-mate Wolfgang von Trips, was killed in the deciding race, the Italian GP at Monza.

Below left Tony Brooks in the Vanwall which he and Stirling Moss drove to victory in the 1957 Grand Prix at Aintree. The car's low-drag body brought new aero-dynamic standards to F1 racing.

Below Phil Hill at Loew's hairpin in the 1961 Monaco Grand Prix in Ferrari's first rear-engined F1 car, the 156 F1, based on the front-engined 256 F1 of 1958. Third at Monaco, Hill took the 1961 drivers' title.

Right Stirling Moss, the winner, in the rear-engined Lotus Climax, leads Richie Ginther (Ferrari 156 F1) around Loew's in the 1961 Monaco GP. Lotus were second that year to Ferrari in the constructors' championship.

Rules and Regulations: 1954–65

Grand-prix and formula racing underwent considerable change during this period of 12 years. The international single-seater formulas adopted were as follows:

1954–7 Capacity limit of 2½ litres unsupercharged or 750 cc supercharged, weight optional. Races to last minimum 3 hours or 500 km (312 miles). Formula 2 suspended.

1958–60 Capacity restrictions as above; racing fuels barred, use of 100–30-octane aviation-grade 'AvGas' compulsory. Race distance cut to 300 km (180 miles) or minimum 2 hours. New unsupercharged 1½-litre Formula 2 introduced.

1959 Production-based single-seater Formula Junior introduced: 1,100 cc push-rod engines, weight minimums 360 kg (790 lb) with 1-litre engine or 400 kg (880 lb) with 1,100 cc.

1961–5 New 1½-litre unsupercharged Formula 1; commercial fuel. Minimum weight 450 kg (990 lb). Enveloping bodies banned. Onboard starters and roll-over driver-protection obligatory. Formula 2 suspended; Formula Junior continued until 1963.

1964–6 New 1-litre Formulas 2 and 3 introduced, replacing Junior. F2 allowed free-design racing engines while F3 allowed only production-based push-rod units.

Below Jim Clark on his way to victory in the 1962 British Grand Prix at Aintree – one of his five wins that year which made him runner-up for the drivers' title. His car was the brilliant Lotus 25 monocoque racer which, in its fuel-injected form, took the title in 1963.

Right *Clark after completing a victory lap following the non-qualifying 1964 British European Auto Racing Grand Prix at Brands Hatch in a Lotus Climax. At right is Lotus chief Colin Chapman.*

Jim Clark (1937–68)

Considered by many to have been the greatest British grand-prix driver of all, Clark began racing in local sprints and sportscar events in the 1950s. His grand-prix career was launched in 1961 when he became top driver for Lotus. His immense talent and his affinity for Colin Chapman's cars became sensationally apparent in December that year when he won the South African, the Natal and the Rand grands prix in the space of 17 days. In 1962 Graham Hill beat him to the title by a whisker after Clark had won the Belgian, British, United States and Mexican grands prix. But the following year Clark was virtually unbeatable in the wonderful Lotus 25: he scored a record seven *grande-épreuve* victories and had clinched the title with three events still to be run! He also took second place in the gruelling Indianapolis 500 race in a mid-engined Lotus-Ford which old hands at the famous 'Brickyard' had dismissed as a toy racer. In 1965 he took the title again – and at Indianapolis he became the first European driver to win the 500 for 45 years, leading for all but 10 of the 200 laps.

For 1966, the first year of the 3-litre formula, Clark had to make do with the 2-litre Lotus while the team's 3-litre units were being prepared. By 1968 Chapman had got the bugs out of what would prove to be an all-conquering car, the Ford-Cosworth DFV-powered Lotus 49, and a seemingly inevitable third title awaited Clark. In April that year, however, in a Formula 2 race at Hockenheim, West Germany, his car skidded off the circuit for still-unexplained reasons, and crashed broadside into a tree. Clark died in hospital shortly afterwards. Of the 72 grands prix he entered, Clark won 25 – better than one in three.

Graham Hill (1929–75)

After working as a driver-mechanic for several seasons Hill became a full-time driver for Lotus in 1958, but lack of success in the notoriously fragile Lotus 16s led to his joining the crisis-torn BRM team the following year. He remained faithful to BRM for six seasons, his patience being rewarded by BRM's only championship, and Hill's first world title, in 1962. For the next three years he was runner-up for the drivers' title, his great rival during this period being Jim Clark. In 1966 Hill won bravely, if somewhat fortuitously, the Indianapolis 500 race (and a considerable fortune) in a Lola-Ford.

The following year he teamed up with Clark to drive the Lotus 49s. Hill had an indifferent season, but in 1968 the car's reliability was transformed and Hill went on to take the drivers' title in the last grand prix of the season. The year 1969 saw him win the Monaco Grand Prix for a record fifth time, but a terrible accident, due to a faulty tyre, almost cost him his life in the United States Grand Prix at Watkins Glen. His legs were badly injured and he never regained his form as a grand-prix driver.

From 1973 onwards he raced his own Cosworth-powered Shadow and Lola grand-prix cars, in 1975 employing Alan Jones and Tony Brise as his top drivers and doing little racing himself. In November of that year, when returning from testing a new car on the Paul Ricard circuit in the south of France, the aircraft Hill was piloting crashed on the northern outskirts of London; Hill, Tony Brise, the team manager, the team designer, and two others were killed.

Left *Graham Hill on 'home' ground – the twisting streets of Monte Carlo, where he won the Monaco Grand Prix five times in seven years (1963–9), coming second and third in the other two years. The picture shows him winning his first Monaco in 1963, driving the BRM with which he had captured the first of his two drivers' titles the previous season.*

ENTER THE MONOCOQUE RACER

The years from 1962 to 1965 (after which the formula changed) saw a series of running battles between Lotus and BRM, with interventions by Ferrari. An all-British outfit, BRM (British Racing Motors), whose leading figures were veteran racing driver Raymond Mays and designer Peter Berthon, had to wait nine years for their first grand-prix victory (the 1959 Dutch race) and another three for their second (the 1962 Dutch); but the latter victory at last opened the floodgates – a total of 11 wins in four seasons. In 1962 the season-long struggle between Graham Hill (BRM) and Jim Clark (Lotus) ended in Hill's favour with his fourth GP win of the season in the South African race. BRM, like Ferrari, designed and built their own engines, transmission, chassis and body; their jewel-like V8 engine, with transistorised ignition and fuel injection, could turn at a (then) astonishing 12,000 rpm.

In 1963 the tables were turned decisively by the Lotus 25, which now added reliability to the superb handling inherent in Colin Chapman's innovative monocoque (chassisless) design, in which the car's structural strength derived from the body-shell components. Clark simply ran away with the championship, clinching the drivers' and constructors' titles while there were still three GPs to run. In the close-run 1964 campaign, Clark had three more victories; but now it was Ferrari's turn. Their updated Dino 156 F1 Aero V8 with semi-monocoque body won the constructors' title and driver John Surtees (an ex-motorcycling champion) took the drivers' title by one point from Graham Hill. Finally, in the last season of the 1½-litre formula, Clark came good again in 1965. The Lotus 25 had given way to the 33, basically similar but with a 32-valve Climax engine, which he drove to six grand-prix victories. By then, such was Chapman's prestige that all the truly competitive works teams were driving cars of monocoque construction.

Jack Brabham (born 1926)

'Black Jack' Brabham arrived in Britain in 1955, having gained experience driving a Cooper-Bristol in his native New South Wales and New Zealand, and that year made his debut in the British Grand Prix at Aintree in a mid-engined Cooper. During the next three seasons he drove almost exclusively for Cooper, taking the Formula 2 title in 1958.

In 1959 Cooper entered its Climax-engined 2½-litre cars in Formula 1 events, winning the championship from Ferrari by a whisker, and Brabham took the drivers' title. The following year he retained his title by winning five grands prix in succession.

The Coopers proved uncompetitive in the 1961 season with the new 1½-litre formula. Brabham now decided to branch out on his own as both driver and constructor, for 1963 signing American Dan Gurney as second driver. The new *équipe* won its first GP (the French) the following year.

In 1966 the hurriedly introduced 3-litre formula caught most of the constructors napping – except for Brabham, who soon had an Australian Repco engine in highly competitive trim. He won four GPs that year, becoming the first driver in history to take the constructors' title in a car of his own design. In the following year, New Zealander Denny Hulme took the drivers' title and clinched the constructors' for Repco-Brabham, while Brabham was runner-up for drivers' honours.

Below *Jack Brabham winning the 1966 British Grand Prix at Brands Hatch in his Repco-Brabham, instantly recognisable by its writhing tangle of exhaust pipes. Brabham was the only team to have a truly race-ready engine for the new 3-litre formula in 1966, the Australian Repco company supplying him with a V8 unit based on a General Motors design (another version of which was used in the Rover V8 road car of the early 1970s).*

THE CIRCUS EXPANDS

Whereas it had been common for the Formula 1 field of the 1950s to comprise perhaps a dozen cars, setting off on a 500km (312-mile) grand prix, the 3-litre era could see as many as 35 cars attempting to qualify for up to 32 grid places in a race of only 250 km (155 miles) or some 90 minutes' duration. This recipe as packaged and sold in the countries of Europe, North America, South America, South Africa and Japan, proved very successful, though many die-hard enthusiasts decried the passing of what they saw as 'proper' grand-prix racing. Today the races vary in length from 253.5 km (157.5 miles) at Detroit to 315.5 km (196.1 miles) at Brands Hatch; and the circuits vary from 3.3 km (2.1 miles) in length at Monaco to 6.9 km (4.3 miles) at Spa-Francorchamps (Belgium). From there being nine World Championship races in 1966, the first year

of the new formula, the class developed to support no fewer than 17 by 1977. That figure is much the same today, though some of the countries staging the races have changed.

Rules and Regulations: 1966–86

For 1966 the FIA's sporting body, the Commission Sportive Internationale (CSI), introduced the 3-litre unblown/1½-litre supercharged formula. Jack Brabham's cars triumphed for the first two years. Thereafter, and for more than a decade, Formula 1 was to be dominated by the Ford-Cosworth DFV V8 engine, used exclusively by Lotus in 1967 and subsequently by a number of teams; it remained virtually unchallenged, except by Ferrari flat-12 power units in the Lauda years (1975–7), until Renault's turbocharged 1½–litre engine achieved reliability at the close of the 1970s.

Above Jackie Stewart in the Ken Tyrrell Matra-Ford MS80 during practice for the 1969 Monaco Grand Prix. The high wings mounted over the rear wheels on the Matra (and on the Lotus-Ford behind it) were banned from the race proper. Stewart retired with a broken drive shaft after leading the race, but went on to take the first of his three drivers' titles that year.

Jackie Stewart (born 1939)

Stewart's serious entry to motor racing came in 1963 after Ken Tyrrell had offered him a test drive in a Formula 3 Cooper-BMC at Goodwood. His rise through Formula 3 and Formula 2 was sensational. In 1964 he won all but two of the Formula 3 races he entered; finished second in his very first Formula 2 race; and in December, while deputising for Jim Clark, he won the second heat of the Formula 1 Rand Grand Prix in South Africa. He instantly became the hottest property among the grand prix rookies, and joined BRM as second driver to Graham Hill for the 1965 season. He won the Italian Grand Prix, was second in the Belgian and Dutch, third at Monaco – and took third place in the drivers' championship behind Clark and Hill.

What promised to be a meteoric rise to the top was interrupted in 1966 when, on a rain-flooded Spa circuit in the Belgian Grand Prix, Stewart's BRM spun off the track. He was rescued by Graham Hill – whose BRM had also crashed – who helped to cut him free from the wrecked car. Stewart had a broken shoulder and a cracked rib.

For 1968, with the BRM in decline, Stewart joined Ken Tyrrell (for whom he had continued to race Formula 2 cars in 1965–7). Tyrrell was now fitting his Matra cars with the Cosworth V8 engine hitherto available only to Lotus. In this first season the Matra-Ford proved fast but not always reliable; Stewart, in addition, broke his wrist in a Formula 2 race at Jarama (Spain) and had to miss a couple of championship-qualifying races. But he won the Dutch Grand Prix at Zandvoort, and followed this by one of his supreme performances, winning the German Grand Prix at the rain- and fog-blanketed Nürburgring by the almost ridiculous margin of four minutes.

The following year the Matra-Ford was almost invincible, Stewart taking the title with six victories. For 1970 Tyrrell used March chassis (Matra requiring theirs for a new V12 engine of their own design) and Stewart won only a single grand prix, the title going to Jochen Rindt (Lotus) with Jacky Ickx (Ferrari) coming second. But in 1971, after early-season failures, Stewart clinched his second title with victories in the Spanish, Monaco, French, British, German, and Canadian grands prix – his win on the tortuous Monaco circuit being achieved without benefit of rear-wheel brakes! After Brazilian Emerson Fittipaldi had taken his first title in 1972, Stewart's third and last title came in 1973 – his fourth place at Monza, after a supremely determined effort following a lengthy pit stop, giving him enough points to frustrate Emerson Fittipaldi's challenge for Lotus.

Stewart's total of 27 *grandes épreuves* (out of 99 starts) was not equalled until Alain Prost won the 1987 Belgian Grand Prix. Like Fangio and Clark before him (and like Niki Lauda in 1975–7) he dominated most of the races he entered so long as his car was up to scratch. Stewart was an heir to the Jack Brabham tradition of technologist drivers. He spent countless hours testing the suspension systems and tyres of his cars and contributed significantly to the art of 'setting-up' racers.

Below *The Ford-Cosworth V8 3-litre engine was the most successful and widely used power unit in the history of Formula 1 racing: its first victory (in its first grand prix) was at the 1967 Dutch GP, when it powered Jim Clark's Lotus 49; its 155th and last victory was in Michele Alboreto's Tyrrell Ford in the Detroit GP of 1983.*

Above James Hunt driving his McLaren-Ford to third place in the Japanese GP, the last race of the season, to secure the 1976 drivers' title. Niki Lauda — who finished one point behind Hunt in the championship — had retired after the second lap, judging rain-lashed Mount Fuji circuit to be unsafe. The race was won by Mario Andretti (Lotus-Ford) from Patrick Depailler (Tyrrell-Ford).

Following two pages Niki Lauda in Casino Square in the Monaco Grand Prix of 1977. He came second to Jody Scheckter, but he went on to take his second world title for Ferrari, in the 312 T2.

THE TURBO REVOLUTION

By the mid-1970s most of the Formula 1 teams – and all the more successful ones except for Ferrari – were using the Cosworth DFV V8 engine. Producing about 410bhp in the 1967 season, the unit was progressively improved until by 1972–4, when Emerson Fittipaldi won two titles and came second to Jackie Stewart in the other, it was pushing out about 480bhp. The Niki Lauda years (*see overleaf*) were interrupted in 1976 by James Hunt, driving for the immensely efficient McLaren team.

Then, in 1977, Renault re-entered the grand-prix scene, bringing with them a 1½-litre turbo-charged V6 engine. Their turbo engine proved extremely fast (and prodigiously thirsty); but it lacked the Cosworth's by now impeccable reliability, and at first the cars lost ground to their more conventional rivals when accelerating out of corners because there was a slight pause ('turbo-lag') before the extra power conferred by the turbo unit took effect. But clearly turbo-charged engines, promising far greater power than normally aspirated ones of twice the capacity, were the Formula 1 power units of the future. (Renault were soon to retire from the Formula 1 scene – but not until they had won the 1979 French Grand Prix, the marque's first victory since Ferenc Szisz's historic triumph 73 years before.)

Tyres were another area of fierce competition. A tyre war between Dunlop, Firestone and Goodyear, which started in 1964, had flared anew in the early years of the 3-litre formula. Dunlop gave up after 1970, as did Firestone at the end of 1974, leaving Goodyear with a monopoly that lasted until Michelin entered the fray in 1978.

Right Renault re-entered grand-prix racing in 1977 with the first Formula 1 turbocharged racers. Their first win was in the 1979 French Grand Prix, with Jean-Pierre Jabouille.

Niki Lauda (born 1949)

From the start of his career in a second-hand Mini-Cooper S, Niki Lauda displayed the ice-cool attitude and iron dedication that would take him to three world drivers' championships.

The tortuous 22.8km (14.2 mile) Nürburgring south of Bonn played a fateful role in his career. In 1969 he made the first-ever nine-minute lap of the circuit in a tiny, ill-handling Formula Vee racer; in 1974 he broke the seven-minute barrier while testing with Ferrari; and in 1975 – the year he won his first drivers' title – he established the all-time record of 6min 58.6sec during practice for the grand prix. The following year he led an unsuccessful campaign to boycott the Nürburgring as being too dangerous for the latest racers. Lauda's warning proved only too prophetic: in that year's grand prix at the 'Ring' his car crashed and caught fire, he breathed in searing fumes, and parts of his face were burnt almost beyond recognition. Lauda hovered between life and death for four days, before making a remarkable recovery to race at Monza only 33 days later.

After winning the title again for Ferrari in 1977, Lauda had three sterile seasons with Brabham and their sick Alfa Romeo engine, then retired.

In 1982 he returned to Formula 1 with McLaren, from whom he won a world-record retainer; he continued with McLaren in 1983 and 1984, when he won his third drivers' title in the last race of the season from team-mate Alain Prost. He retired for good in 1985.

Lauda's will to win and his obsession with the finer details of cars and circuits helped to make him one of the great test drivers of the past two decades.

Right Lauda's 1978 protective gear included this all-enveloping helmet over a fire-resistant head-mask; a fresh-air pipe enabled him to breathe freely in event of a fire.

INNOVATION

The 1960s and 1970s saw major advances in the design and construction of grand-prix cars. Tyres altered most visibly in width, and by the end of the 1970s the maximum wheel width permitted, 21in (550mm), led to the use of enormous rear tyres. It became customary for the front and rear tyres to be made of different compounds to improve handling; indeed, those of the two front wheels also often differed because, with races run clockwise around all the circuits, the front left tyre was subject to greater loads and wear. And then, of course, special tyres were developed for the practice sessions; and different treads were used for wet and dry conditions.

The most important design advance of the 1960s was the elimination of the chassis in favour of a monocoque (stressed-skin) structure in which the load-bearing body consisted of 'boxes' of riveted alloy sheet strengthened laterally at points along the hull. The chief strengthening elements were the floorpan, the dash panel in front of the steering wheel, the bulkhead between the driving seat and the engine, and the mountings for the suspension. The body was both stiffer and lighter than that of previous cars. In such designs even the engine acted as a stressed member and was bolted onto the rearmost box; and at least one of the suspension arms was attached to the engine casing. The first truly successful realisation of this idea was Colin Chapman's Lotus 25. The car made its debut at the 1962 Dutch Grand Prix, won five GPs that year and, in 1963, enabled Jim Clark to take the drivers' title and Lotus to clinch their first ever Constructors' Championship.

Chapman, the most innovative designer in the field of grand-prix aerodynamics and suspension systems during this period, stunned the racing world again with his 'ground-effect' Lotus 79, with which Mario Andretti and Ronnie Peterson ran away with first and second places in the drivers' championship in 1978. Ground effect involved smoothing the under-car surfaces and attaching 'skirts' to the car sides in order to give the underside the profile of a saucer. This shape had the effect of creating a vacuum between the car and the road surface, the effect increasing with the speed of the car. The vacuum 'sucked' the car down onto the road, enabling it to corner at speeds that hitherto would have been inconceivable. This radically increased performance put great strain on the structural integrity of the cars — but perhaps even greater strain on the drivers, few of whom were sorry when ground-effect designs were banned at the end of the 1982 season.

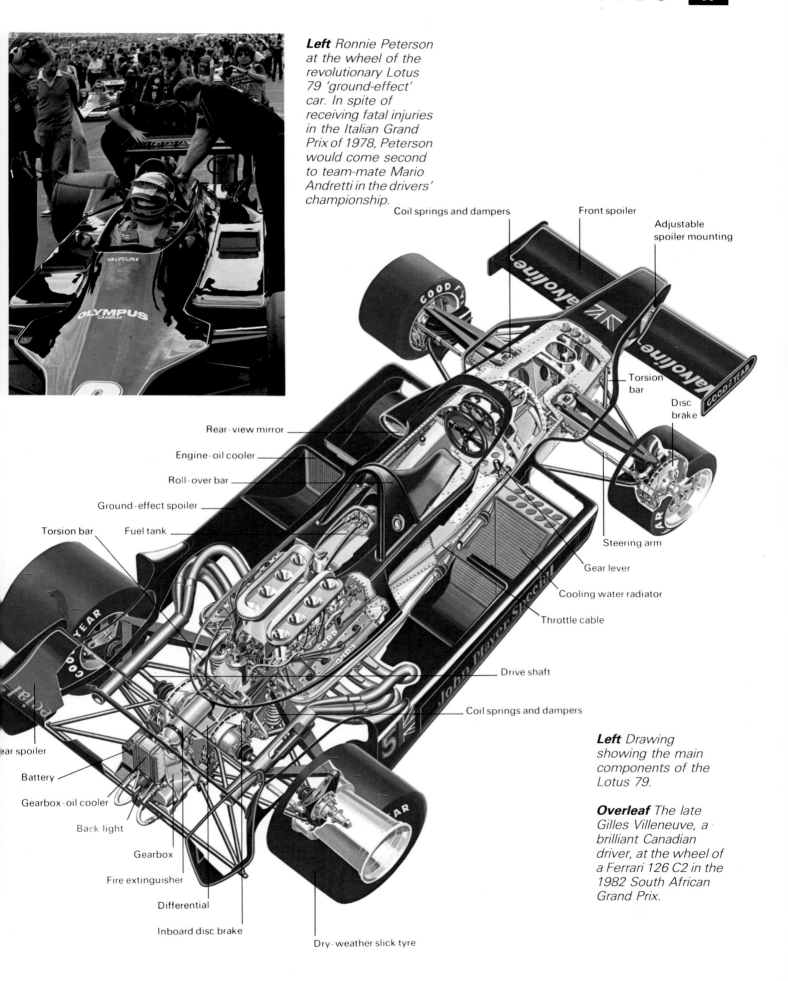

Left *Ronnie Peterson at the wheel of the revolutionary Lotus 79 'ground-effect' car. In spite of receiving fatal injuries in the Italian Grand Prix of 1978, Peterson would come second to team-mate Mario Andretti in the drivers' championship.*

Coil springs and dampers

Front spoiler

Adjustable spoiler mounting

Torsion bar

Disc brake

Rear-view mirror

Engine-oil cooler

Roll-over bar

Ground-effect spoiler

Torsion bar

Fuel tank

Steering arm

Gear lever

Cooling water radiator

Throttle cable

Drive shaft

Coil springs and dampers

Rear spoiler

Battery

Gearbox-oil cooler

Back light

Gearbox

Fire extinguisher

Differential

Inboard disc brake

Dry-weather slick tyre

Left *Drawing showing the main components of the Lotus 79.*

Overleaf *The late Gilles Villeneuve, a brilliant Canadian driver, at the wheel of a Ferrari 126 C2 in the 1982 South African Grand Prix.*

Formula 1 Drivers' Championship 1950–86 Winners and Runners-up

1950 Giuseppe Farina (Alfa Romeo)
Juan Manuel Fangio (Alfa Romeo)

1951 Juan Manuel Fangio (Alfa Romeo)
Alberto Ascari (Ferrari)

1952 Alberto Ascari (Ferrari)
Giuseppe Farina (Ferrari)

1953 Alberto Ascari (Ferrari)
Juan Manuel Fangio (Maserati)

1954 Juan Manuel Fangio (Maserati/
Mercedes-Benz)
Froilan Gonzalez (Ferrari)

1955 Juan Manuel Fangio (Mercedes-Benz)
Stirling Moss (Mercedes-Benz)

1956 Juan Manuel Fangio (Ferrari)
Stirling Moss (Maserati)

1957 Juan Manuel Fangio (Maserati)
Stirling Moss (Vanwall)

1958 Mike Hawthorn (Ferrari)
Stirling Moss (Vanwall)

1959 Jack Brabham (Cooper-Climax)
Tony Brooks (Ferrari)

1960 Jack Brabham (Cooper-Climax)
Bruce McLaren (Cooper-Climax)

1961 Phil Hill (Ferrari)
Wolfgang von Trips (Ferrari)

1962 Graham Hill (BRM)
Jim Clark (Lotus-Climax)

1963 Jim Clark (Lotus-Climax)
Graham Hill (BRM)

1964 John Surtees (Ferrari)
Graham Hill (BRM)

1965 Jim Clark (Lotus-Climax)
Graham Hill (BRM)

1966	Jack Brabham (Repco-Brabham) John Surtees (Ferrari/Cooper-Maserati)	1977	Niki Lauda (Ferrari) Jody Scheckter (Wolf-Ford)
1967	Denny Hulme (Repco-Brabham) Jack Brabham (Repco-Brabham)	1978	Mario Andretti (Lotus-Ford) Ronnie Peterson (Lotus-Ford)
1968	Graham Hill (Lotus-Ford) Jackie Stewart (Matra-Ford)	1979	Jody Scheckter (Ferrari) Gilles Villeneuve (Ferrari)
1969	Jackie Stewart (Matra-Ford) Jacky Ickx (Ferrari)	1980	Alan Jones (Williams-Ford) Nelson Piquet (Brabham-Ford)
1970	Jochen Rindt (Lotus-Ford) Jacky Ickx (Ferrari)	1981	Nelson Piquet (Brabham-Ford) Carlos Reutemann (Williams-Ford)
1971	Jackie Stewart (Tyrrell-Ford) Ronnie Peterson (March-Ford)	1982	Keke Rosberg (Williams-Ford) Didier Pironi (Ferrari) & John Watson (McLaren-Ford)
1972	Emerson Fittipaldi (Lotus-Ford) Jackie Stewart (Tyrrell-Ford)	1983	Nelson Piquet (Brabham-BMW) Alain Prost (Renault)
1973	Jackie Stewart (Tyrrell-Ford) Emerson Fittipaldi (Lotus-Ford)	1984	Niki Lauda (McLaren-TAG) Alain Prost (McLaren-TAG)
1974	Emerson Fittipaldi (McLaren-Ford) Clay Regazzoni (Ferrari)	1985	Alain Prost (McLaren-TAG) Michele Alboreto (Ferrari)
1975	Niki Lauda (Ferrari) Emerson Fittipaldi (McLaren-Ford)	1986	Alain Prost (McLaren-TAG) Nigel Mansell (Williams-Honda)
1976	James Hunt (McLaren-Ford) Niki Lauda (Ferrari)		

TEAMS, CARS AND DRIVERS

CREATING A WINNER

Below Williams team engineers working on a Honda F1 engine in the pit area prior to 1987 practice and qualifying sessions at Río's Jacarepagua circuit.

The road to developing a grand-prix winner is long and difficult, strewn with potential pitfalls set to catch out many hopeful racing-car designers. From the moment an idea begins to germinate in a designer's mind to the day the gleaming machine is pushed out into a pit lane to make its first test run, the works team will be operating flat-out in every department. Creating a car that will compete is comparatively straightforward: creating a winner is something else again.

NEW SHAPES
AND MATERIALS

Until the end of the 1970s the technology of grand-prix car construction had remained little changed for more than a decade. Basically the drivers sat in 'cigars' made from aluminium alloy sheets rivetted together to enclose fuel tanks, piping and other accessories. But aerospace technology brought with it remarkable innovations such as carbon fibre, which combines great strength and remarkable lightness, and this is now the material from which every F1 racing-car chassis is made.

Working with such materials is extremely expensive, increasing the pressure on designers to make certain everything is 'right first time'. But the chassis design is an integral part of the completed car, so there may be features which the designer would like to incorporate, but is prevented from doing by other considerations.

In the days of the normally aspirated engines (until the mid-1970s) you could build an ultra-slim monocoque body hardly any wider than the Ford–Cosworth DFV V8 engine that was used by most of the grand-prix teams from the late 1960s onwards. But that was only in theory. You still needed to 'package-in' as much fuel as possible and, until the advent of a 'central' single fuel-cell immediately behind the driver, designers had fuel tanks on either side of the cockpit as well.

Once the central fuel-cell became the accepted style, other considerations prevented the evolution of pencil-slim grand-prix cars. Where were the radiators to go? In the nose section, perhaps, ahead of the drivers' feet? But that would have made the cockpit intolerably hot. What's more, radiators are heavy components, so from the point of view of the car's overall balance, the best home for them is somewhere towards the centre of the car. Hence the appearance of 'pods' on either side of the cockpit during the mid-1970s.

The next constraint on designers' talents came in the form of turbocharged engines. Although these engines were no bigger than their predecessors, the associated paraphernalia of piping, compressors and intercoolers meant that packaging a turbocharged power unit into a chassis became an unusually complex task. Fifteen years of using the Ford–Cosworth DFV had made engine installation a pretty routine affair. Now there were several brand-new turbo engines on the scene – but very little in the way of data on how they should be mated to the chassis.

Williams designer Patrick Head was faced with precisely this problem in the middle of 1983. One of the last of the top Formula 1 teams to switch from normally aspirated Ford engines, Williams signed a deal with Honda for the exclusive use of the company's turbo F1 engine. But Head had to start from scratch, with precious little technical input even from Honda, who were as new to the problem of turbo installation as Williams.

Left Patrick Head, Williams' designer, conferring with team driver Nelson Piquet after practice for the 1987 Brazilian Grand Prix at Río.

Pages 50–1 Alain Prost aboard the McLaren-TAG on his way to victory in the 1987 Brazilian GP.

When Honda delivered its first engine to Williams' factory at Didcot (Oxfordshire) it was, literally, just that — an engine. Head and his design team had to work out, through trial and error, the best positions for the turbochargers, exhaust pipes and intercoolers. It sounds a fairly routine problem: in fact it took three seasons to perfect, but it culminated in the splendid Williams FW11 which won 9 out of 16 races during 1986 in the hands of Nigel Mansell and Nelson Piquet. Then, when Honda decided to supply engines to a second team in 1987, Lotus was presented with the whole engine installation 'on a plate'. Three seasons of intensive Williams development was, in effect, handed straight over to a rival, saving Lotus an enormous amount of effort, not to mention money. It was frustrating for Patrick Head, but just one of those quirks of racing fortune which crop up from time to time.

Very seldom do designers get the opportunity to produce an entire chassis–engine package from scratch — apart, that is, from those at Ferrari whose enormous (Fiat-funded) resources mean that the famous Italian team never needs to stint on any aspect of technical detail. Nonetheless, the most spectacular example in recent times of a designer starting with a completely clean sheet of paper was the superb series of TAG turbo-engined McLarens which powered Niki Lauda and Alain Prost to the world championship in 1984 and 1985/6 respectively.

In 1982, shortly after Lauda's emergence from retirement, the McLaren team gave its chief designer John Barnard a totally free hand to produce a turbocharged F1 winner. An arrangement had been forged with Porsche to build the new engine, with backing from the Franco-Saudi high-technology group Techniques d'Avant Garde (TAG); but while the German company put its vast technical know-how into the project, it was Barnard who decided on the engine's basic configuration, mindful of the need to install it into a chassis.

The result was one of the neatest and most homogeneous F1 machines ever seen. Throughout the design process there had been very little

Left *Ayrton Senna in the 1987 Lotus. Powered by the Honda engine hitherto exclusive to the Williams team, the Lotus was the first car to exploit the radically new 'active-ride' suspension, giving constant ride-height under all loads.*

compromise; everything in the chassis, engine and gearbox was tailor-made to work in harmony. Small wonder, then, that basically the same McLaren–TAG formula was still winning races in 1987.

Aerodynamic excellence has been one of the McLaren–TAG's strongest points. By having control of every aspect of the car's design. Barnard ensured that the air flow over the rear of the car was as unimpeded as possible, providing maximum downforce with the minimum possible drag. Others have not been so lucky over the past few years.

In 1985 Ferrari completely re-designed the turbocharger system on its wide-angle V6 engine in order to improve the aerodynamics of its new car. Until then, the Ferrari's turbos were mounted on top of the engine within the 'vee' formed by the two banks of cylinders. As a result a high engine cover was needed and this, in turn, interfered with the airflow over the rear wing. With the turbos repositioned low down on either side of the engine, below the arms of the 'vee', the engine cover could be lowered, and the car's aerodynamics improved.

Over at the Brabham team, its long-time de-signer Gordon Murray faced a similar problem at the end of 1984. Architect of a succession of impressive grand-prix cars, the innovative Murray designs had been compromised since 1982 by the shape of the powerful four-cylinder BMW turbo engine. The BMW unit had a tall cylinder block, so that when installed in the 1985 BT54 chassis, it too required a rather high engine cover. In turn, the cover partly masked the rear wing, reducing its effectiveness. Murray hit on a novel plan to get over this problem when designing the new BT55. But, as so often happens when designers stray from conventional courses, what looked like a world-beater on paper turned into a disaster out on the circuits. Determined to improve the car's aerodynamics, Murray collaborated with BMW to develop a purpose-built engine laid over at an angle of 70 degrees. This enabled the car to be dramatically low, its rear wing operating in much clearer air, and pre-season opinions suggested it would be a success. Unfortunately, it wasn't. The angled engine never delivered the same performance as the upright unit it had replaced. In addition, the car had poor traction, and its drivers hated the low cockpit, which obliged them to drive with their chins

Opposite page *Alain Prost's McLaren-TAG MP4/3 in 'topless' form before the 1987 Belgian Grand Prix. The matt-black chassis is made from carbon fibre. The quickly removable, usually one-piece, body shell is little more than an aerodynamic envelope.*

Below *Working on the McLaren-TAG MP4/3 engine in the pits at Río's Jacarepagua circuit.*

tucked down on their chests. So, although the Brabham BT55's aerodynamic efficiency could be proved by reference to the speeds achieved on certain sections of certain circuits, it failed for other reasons to achieve any worthwhile race results. At the end of the year it was scrapped, to be replaced the following season by a more conventional-looking car, though still with the 'angled' BMW engine.

Interestingly, grand-prix cars often reflect the personality of their designers. The late Colin Chapman's cars were crisply to the point, brilliantly innovative, yet amazingly straightforward. He had a rare, intuitive talent that solved technical conundrums with a flash of genius. You were left wondering, if it really was that simple, why nobody had done it before. Of course, it never *was* simple: Chapman just had the gift of making it *look* like that.

Similarly, Gordon Murray's artistic inclination could be seen in the lines of his more successful Brabhams, as could Patrick Head's solid, if conservative, commonsense approach in a succession of Williams designs which have regularly won races over the past decade.

During his days at McLaren, John Barnard developed a reputation for demanding uncompromisingly high standards from all those who worked around him, and he himself lavished infinite care on his designs. Throughout the early 1980s the McLaren cars wanted for nothing in terms of material excellence. It cost money, of course, but in that respect the McLaren team was fortunate: while Barnard was a brilliant designer, his fellow McLaren director Ron Dennis proved wondrously adept at securing the enormous financial backing necessary to keep the show on the road.

Below Riccardo Patrese, Brabham-BMW's number one driver in 1986. He was joined by Derek Warwick after Elio de Angelis was killed while high-speed testing the BT55 at the Paul Ricard circuit – which as a result was considerably shortened for the French Grand Prix two months later. For 1988, Patrese signed to Williams-Judd.

Of course, before the first prototype is built, many hours will have been spent considering its aerodynamic specification in the most minute detail. Twenty years ago, F1 designers would put models, with tufts of cotton wool or pieces of string tacked to them, into wind tunnels to study the effects of airflow over a car – a far cry from the computer-controlled techniques employed today.

Aerodynamic testing is virtually a full-time occupation for highly qualified members of the top teams. It is not necessary, though, for John Barnard to stand watching each individual wind-tunnel test in order to reach a conclusion about an individual aspect of the design process. He can sit behind his desk in Guildford and study a computer print-out sent to him directly from the Ferrari wind tunnel at Maranello. That will tell him everything that he could have learned on a two-day trip to Italy.

ENGINE
CONFIGURATIONS

As far as engine configuration during the turbo era is concerned, only TAG and Ferrari really started with an absolutely clean drawing board. Other engine makers have not been in a position

of such luxury. For example, Honda's V6 configuration evolved from their successful F2 engines which dominated the European Championship in the early 1980s. BMW's four-cylinder engine has an even longer pedigree, for although it, too, was derived from an F2 unit, its ultimate origins are in the production-based touring-car units which were used as long ago as the early 1960s. Brian Hart's small factory at Harlow did a brilliant job developing its Ford-based four-cylinder turbo unit which was used by the Toleman (now Benetton) team until the end of 1985. Hart's engine was based on the light-alloy Formula 2 engine which propelled Toleman to the 1980 European Championship and which in turn evolved from technology culled from Hart's development expertise with Ford-based racing engines over the previous decade.

In 1986, when Ford decided on a completely new F1 assault, it turned again to Cosworth Engineering to produce a brand-new turbo from the ground up. The result was a compact, wide-angle V6 which, in 1987, found itself installed in the super-slim Benetton B187 designed by Rory Byrne. By common agreement among his rivals, Byrne's latest package is one of the most aerodynamically impressive to be seen this season. Achieving the lowest possible drag without losing too much downforce is the crucial equation which governs F1 at the present time: striking the most effective balance between the

Opposite page The V6 engine in the 1987 Ferrari. The team were hoping for greater reliability from their turbocharging unit after a disappointing 1986 season.

Below The Ford-Cosworth DFZ V-8 engine in the 1987 Tyrrell. With the withdrawal of the Renault V6 turbo from F1 at the end of 1986, Tyrrell decided to concentrate on normally aspirated engines.

two is the elusive target of every designer in the game.

Alfa Romeo and Motori Moderni opted for V8 and V6 configurations respectively. Alfa never seemed to be quite certain how it wanted to conduct its F1 involvement. Initially it forged a link with Brabham from 1976–9; then it built and ran its own team of cars until the end of 1985, when it decided to miss a year's racing while development proceeded with a brand-new four-cylinder engine. A contract was signed with Ligier for its use in 1987, but the whole project screeched to a halt after the French team's number-one driver René Arnoux made some outspoken comments about the engine during a test session in Italy. Alfa Romeo promptly withdrew from racing, thereby ending a somewhat patchy period of achievement.

The Motori Moderni company is a tiny Italian firm which was originally established to build turbo engines for the equally small Minardi team. Although it is unlikely actually to win a grand prix, the combination of Minardi and Motori Moderni has proved that it is possible to compete in F1 without access to the enormous budgets consumed by the established front-line teams.

TESTING
THE NEW CAR

All these teams and engine manufacturers eventually, of course, reach the moment of truth. After months of planning, chasing tardy component suppliers, ensuring that tyres have been delivered, double-checking that all the piping and wiring has been completed correctly, the time comes to start the engine and see if the whole thing works. To start with, the engine is run at little more than tick-over speed in the factory. As it warms up for the first time, mechanics will be examining it in minute detail, ensuring there are no unexpected leaks or obvious malfunctions. It will be warmed up to operating temperature and then switched off. It is likely that the car is then stripped down and rebuilt once more, before

Main picture *Rory Byrne's impressive Benetton B187, in action at the 1987 Brazilian Grand Prix. The car's shape successfully created downforce while retaining excellent aerodynamic properties.*

Inset *Ford's other Formula 1 engine, a turbocharged wide-angle V6, was first raced, as the THL2, in the 1986 Lola. The 1987 version seen here powered the Benetton. For 1988 the team chose non-turbo Ford power – the short-block DFR.*

being taken to a circuit for its 'shakedown' run.

Finding a circuit available at the right time can be a major problem. Most British-based grand-prix teams have their new F1 cars ready for testing at the same time, in February or March. As a result, they have to go abroad to get a chance of any serious pre-season testing, since Silverstone, Brands Hatch and Donington Park are all too frequently covered with ice or snow at this time of year. Occasionally it is possible to find a decent day on which to run the car round for a few laps, but for winter testing most teams rely on the Circuit Paul Ricard, just inland from Bandol (between Marseille and Toulon), Jerez in south-west Spain, or Estoril in Portugal. Of course, there is no absolute guarantee of good weather anywhere in Europe, so there is always a 'communal' F1 test week at Río de Janeiro a month or so before the season opens with the Brazilian Grand Prix.

Assuming the car runs reliably for, say, 30 or 40 laps, the team can start thinking seriously in terms of getting down to some really high-speed testing. In most cases the drivers will be taking things easy at first – not because they have any doubts about the car's structural integrity, but because the designers and engineers have asked them to keep an eye on the instruments, to report oil pressure, temperature and so-on. Running gently – say five seconds or so off a really competitive time – the car will probably feel pretty good. But it is only when a top driver begins to run close to racing speed that potential problems begin to make themselves known.

The role of a racing driver in the test and development process is absolutely crucial. Although recent years have seen the use of computers to monitor engine performance, fuel-consumption and turbo-boost pressure from the pit wall, not to mention pit-to-car radio communication, ultimately a car's success depends on the driver: there is no substitute for seat-of-the-pants judgement. The most minor technical change can produce a quite violent effect on the car's performance. But only a driver can describe accurately what is happening out on the circuit.

As an example, let us go back to 1978. That gifted and versatile American Mario Andretti was then at the peak of his F1 achievement, poised to clinch the World Championship with the superb ground-effect Lotus 79. Prior to the

Right The cramped cockpit of a modern F1 car: Alain Prost waits while engineers adjust the front suspension of his McLaren before a 1987 practice session.

Austrian Grand Prix, he was trying his Lotus on the very fast Österreichring circuit, carrying out comparative tests between two outwardly identical cars. One was superb, hugging the track 'like a white line', to use Mario's own words. The other was awful: it felt erratic and unstable. By the end of the day Andretti was almost tearing his hair out in frustration as he tried to get to the bottom of the problem. It seemed insoluble.

Eventually, the engineers and mechanics went through the car's detail specification with a fine-tooth comb. There was only one difference between the two machines. One had a front lower suspension arm of a slightly different shape to the other car. It was changed and, hey presto, the 'rogue' car suddenly felt as safe and secure as its stablemate. The different profile of the suspension arm, stuck out in the air stream, was affecting the airflow under the car and badly upsetting its balance. From such tiny adjustments are race winners produced!

Of course, some drivers would never have noticed! The late lamented Ronnie Peterson, one of the greatest drivers of the post-war era, was, frankly, a hopeless test driver. But he had such a towering talent, terrific speed and split-second reflexes that, in many cases, it didn't matter. Ronnie could extract every ounce of potential from any racing car he sat in, often 'driving through' any handling imbalance to produce a tremendous race result. But such an approach was not always to the long-term benefit of the team.

ACTIVE SUSPENSION

The single most innovative technical development of 1987, which looked certain to have considerable long-term impact on F1 technology, was the arrival on the scene of computer-controlled suspension systems capable of smoothing out the bumps and ripples on the track surface, giving the driver an easier ride and in

Above The front aerofoil and suspension of Piquet's 1987 Williams-Honda. Both could be finely adjusted when setting up the car for a particular circuit.

Right The rear wing of the 1987 Benetton-Ford. Handling of F1 cars depends critically on the way the air passes over the car's body and onto the wing surfaces.

general aiding the car's aerodynamic balance.

Team Lotus had been working on such a project behind the scenes for more than five years, mindful of its potential road-car application, but only when Ayrton Senna tried it on the prototype Lotus-Honda 99T for the first time was the green light given for its adoption throughout the team's 1987 F1 programme.

Basically, 'active suspension', as it was termed, fulfilled the same function as the muscles and sensory system in a human being. Just as one instantly adjusts one's stance to a level footing on bumpy ground, so the active suspension system reacts to undulations on the race track surface in milli-seconds, adjusting the suspension on the one or more corners of the car which may be affected.

Controlled by a central computer mounted beneath the seat of the Lotus 99T, the system receives input from a system of sensors all over the car, immediately interpreting those messages and transmitting a reaction to the hydraulic jacks which replace the conventional coil springs in such a system. The benefits are more consistent handling and reduced driver fatigue, factors which helped Senna to win both the 1987 Monaco and Detroit Grands Prix in storming style.

However, although cost and complexity obliged Team Lotus to shelve the system in 1988, the rival Williams équipe has developed a similar 'reactive' system, which was fitted to the car used by Nelson Piquet to win the 1987 Italian Grand Prix. Suitably refined and updated, it was installed as 'standard equipment' on the Williams-Judd FW12s raced by Nigel Mansell and Riccardo Patrese in 1988. Several other teams, including Benetton and Ferrari, were known to be toying with similar systems for possible introduction later in 1988. This, overwhelmingly, is the area where future F1 technical development promises to run at a tremendously competitive pitch.

1988 ENGINE
DEVELOPMENT

Grand prix engine development was mid-way through a transitional phase in 1988 with a view to banning turbocharged engines completely by the end of the season. Restricted to 4-bar boost pressure in 1987, the performance of the turbos was capped still further at the start of 1988 by the imposition of a 2.5-bar boost-pressure limit and a reduction in their fuel allowance from 195

Above For 1988 the Williams team installed the normally aspirated Judd engine, a 3.5-litre V8 used also by Ligier and March.

Opposite Alain Prost surveys the Honda engine newly installed in the 1988 McLaren MP4/4.

to 150 litres. The idea was to create parity of performance between the turbos and their naturally aspirated rivals, but the ease with which Alain Prost dominated the first race of the year in Brazil at the wheel of the new McLaren-Honda MP4/4 suggested that, even with these new power restrictions, the Japanese V6s could still develop around 670bhp – which certainly looked enough to get the job done.

Honda turbos powered both Lotus and McLaren in 1988, the latter team replacing Williams as the Japanese motor giant's prestige front runner. Williams therefore turned to English specialist engineer John Judd for the supply of a band-new naturally aspirated 3.5-litre, four-valves-per-cylinder V8 (ironically, this engine was developed from a unit originally commissioned by Honda for use in a 3-litre F1 in 1982 but shelved in favour of their turbo project). Judd has a lengthy race-engineering pedigree stretching back to the early 1960s, when he was apprenticed with Coventry-Climax and he later worked on the Australian Repco V8 F1 units which powered Jack Brabham's team cars to the World Championship in 1976–7.

The arrival of Judd's engine on the scene helped considerably with the shift of emphasis to naturally aspirated engines, hitherto the preserve mainly of Cosworth Engineering, who would otherwise have been snowed under with orders for their DFZ-derived units. Judd was also supplying Ligier and March, while Benetton, Ford's leading runner, had switched from the Cosworth-built turbo to the short–block DFR, another 3.5-litre derivative of the DFZ. The DFZ also replaced Motori-Moderni V6 turbo power at Minardi, as well as powering newcomers from Dallara, EuroBrun and Coloni. The aged Alfa turbo continued to stagger on, powering the Osella, while Zakspeed retained its four-cylinder turbo and Arrows its Megatron turbo.

Right The Ferrari F186 (i.e. F1, 1986), with number one driver Michele Alboreto aboard. The aerial shot shows clearly the shape of the front and rear aerofoils, the side pods and the aerodynamic body shell. The Ferrari team relies on prodigious financial backing from Fiat.

FOUR
SUPERSTARS

Alain Prost

Alain Prost, born on 28 February 1955 in the provincial town of St-Chamond, near Lyon, displayed the Midas touch from the very start of his career. He won the 1973 World Karting Championship and three years later dominated the European Formula Renault series, while in 1979 he took the European Formula 3 championship. The way was clearly open to grand-prix stardom. Offered a test drive for McLaren at the end of the 1979 season, he was signed on the spot by team director Teddy Mayer.

Alain scored a championship point on his F1 debut in the Argentine Grand Prix, but his first season proved generally disappointing. For 1981 he switched to Renault and immediately began to reel off victories. Yet the drivers' title eluded him, the Renault suffering a succession of mechanical failures. Finally, a major disagreement with the team saw him quit Renault at the end of the 1983 season.

When John Watson left McLaren, there was a vacancy in the team alongside Niki Lauda and Prost took it with hardly a moment's hesitation. It was absolutely the right choice. With its new Porsche-built TAG turbo engine now ready to race, the 1984 McLaren proved to be in a class of its own; but although Alain won seven races to Niki's five, the latter took the title by half a point.

In 1985 Prost made no mistakes, winning five grands-prix to clinch his long-awaited championship. His amazingly smooth driving style and mechanical empathy have marked him out as the natural successor to Lauda as the best F1 'technocrat', but his speed and consistency are such that he is now regarded as superior even to the famous Austrian. When Prost repeated the title-winning feat in the last race of the 1986 season, he became the first man to win two titles in a row since Jack Brabham in 1959 and 1960.

In 1987, lack of development on the TAG/Porsche engine left Prost with a distinct performance handicap, but he drove brilliantly throughout the year. Three grand prix victories came his way. At Estoril he relentlessly hounded Gerhard Berger into a spin only three laps from the chequered flag, surging through to beat Jackie Stewart's record of 27 wins which had endured for 13 years.

Right After a
relatively modest
1987 season, Alain
Prost swiftly
re-emphasised his
credentials by taking
three of the first four
GPs of 1988, his
McLaren MP4/4
(below) transformed
by the prepotent
Honda engine.

Nelson Piquet

If his father's ambitions had prevailed, Nelson Piquet might well have scaled the heights of international tennis instead of getting involved in motor racing. Born in Río de Janeiro on 17 August 1952, Nelson initially followed in his father's footsteps and became an accomplished teenage tennis player before the lure of cars, karts and motorcycles swayed his ambitions.

After graduating quickly through the domestic Formula Super Vee class, Nelson set out for Europe at the start of 1977 to begin an international Formula 3 campaign. At the wheel of a Ralt, he limbered up by finishing third in the European Championship, preparing the way for 1978 when he took the British domestic Formula 3 scene by storm. Winning 13 races during that season, he had clinched the BP Championship before the last round, attracting a lot of interest from Formula 1 team managers in the process. He was invited to drive for the Ensign team in the German Grand Prix, where he retired, before going on to handle a private McLaren in the Austrian, Dutch and Italian races. In the last event of the year, the Canadian Grand Prix, he drove a works Brabham for the first time, laying the groundwork for a partnership which would last seven years.

After Niki Lauda retired abruptly (albeit temporarily) late in 1979, Piquet found himself elevated to team leader at the age of 27. In 1980, at the wheel of a new Ford-engined Brabham, he won his first grand prix at Long Beach (California), and went on to score triumphs in the Dutch and Italian races. Despite his novice status, he finished runner-up in the World Championship to Alan Jones.

The 1981 season saw him win his first World Championship, edging out Carlos Reutemann by a single point in a nail-biting finale at Las Vegas. Then for 1982 the Brabham team switched to BMW turbo power, which gave Piquet a mechanically troubled season with only one win. But he bounced back to snatch his second championship in 1983 after a close struggle with Alain Prost's Renault. Two relatively bleak years followed, after which he stunned the Formula 1 world by switching to the Williams–Honda squad for 1986 after Brabham boss Bernie Ecclestone failed to offer him the financial deal he wanted. Piquet came close to taking the Championship again in 1986, being eased out by Alain Prost only in the very last race of the year.

With eight years of grand-prix experience under his belt, Nelson remains as firmly committed to his chosen sport as he was when he started. Yet his intuitive skill is sometimes compromised by inconsistent performances and the occasional lapse. The way in which he ruled the roost at Río, Hockenheim and Monza in 1986 contrasted starkly with lacklustre outings at both Monaco and Estoril.

Although eclipsed by Nigel Mansell in terms of pure speed, Nelson's tactical approach to the 1987 World Championship paid dividends as he edged through to take his third title with more than a passing degree of good fortune. Off-track, however, Piquet was unhappy at Williams, and for 1988 signed a Lotus contract – a move which contributed to Williams losing their Honda engine supply.

Off-track, he has no interest in socialising with the motor-racing crowd and carries out only the bare minimum of promotional work for his sponsors. An assessment of Nelson's place in the F1 hall of fame will have to wait a few years yet for, despite those inconsistencies, this brilliant if moody Brazilian plans to race on for several more years.

Opposite The 1988 Lotus-Honda 100T. Lotus's new man, Nelson Piquet, familiar with Honda power and, since mid-1987, with active suspension in the Williams, had high hopes of his change of scene.

Above 1987 World Champion Piquet in his new Lotus strip. In early 1988 he spent nine days, and about 1500 miles, testing the Lotus at the Río circuit, followed by further sessions at Imola.

Nigel Mansell

If sheer determination alone won world championships, Nigel Mansell would have had a stranglehold on the title for the past five years. Off-track a devoted family man, once he gets behind the wheel of a grand-prix car an all-consuming passion for success powers his whole being.

Mansell's career began at Lucas Aerospace, where he worked on a number of projects including the RB211 jet engine, and later became a senior sales engineer at Girling before taking up motor-racing full-time. After graduating from the cut-and-thrust world of kart racing, Mansell won his first Formula Ford race at Mallory Park in 1976, and it was only another three years before he got his first F1 test, for the Lotus team, at the Paul Ricard circuit in the south of France.

His dogged exploits in Formula Ford and later Formula 3 had been brought to the attention of Lotus boss Colin Chapman, who Mansell im-

pressed considerably in that first F1 test. He was signed on as test and development driver for 1980 and, in the Austrian Grand Prix, was given the chance to handle a third car. Typical of his determination, he drove for much of the race in pain from petrol burns after the fuel cell split, but he refused to retire until the engine blew up.

In 1981 he was recruited full-time to the Lotus grand-prix line-up and had several promising races. But Team Lotus fortunes were at a low ebb at this time and grand-prix success continually eluded him. Chapman's faith in his talent never wavered, but the Lotus boss died suddenly from a heart attack in December 1982, and Mansell lost a valuable friend and mentor just when he needed him most.

Nigel stayed with Lotus to the end of the 1984 season; but there were times when his driving displayed a slightly desperate quality as he tried, time and again, to win his first grand prix. Success was not to come his way until 1985, after he had left Team Lotus to sign for the Williams team as second driver to Keke Rosberg.

Just as his critics were confirming their view that Mansell would never win a Formula 1 race, he triumphed in the Grand Prix of Europe at Brands Hatch. Then he won the next race in South Africa, to end the season in sixth place in the championship. He had mounted the springboard to success at last. In 1986, riding high on the crest of a wave of self-confidence, Mansell sped to five grand-prix triumphs. He lost his chance of winning the championship only when a tyre failed at maximum speed in the last race of the season. But Mansell by then had established himself as a world-class driver.

It was more of the same for Mansell throughout 1987, a heady blend of breathtaking speed spiced with a handful of unfortunate driving errors and not the best of the breaks on the mechanical side. After winning six races in stupendous style, a practice accident at Suzuka two days before the Japanese Grand Prix wrote the dogged Englishman out of the championship script with two races left to run, handing the title unchallenged to his unloved team-mate Piquet.

Opposite page *Nigel Mansell, in 1988 colours (and upper lip), was hoping for better luck after two brilliant but misfortune-dogged seasons.*

Below *His new mount, the Williams-Judd FW12, seen here on test at Río, seemed the quickest of 1988's non-turbo cars – but could it compete with the resurgent McLarens?*

Right Ayrton Senna, after a curate's-egg 1987 with Lotus, seemed likely to transform his career in McLaren colours.

Ayrton Senna

Below *The McLaren-Honda MP4/4 opened the 1988 season sensationally, waltzing away with the first six races, Senna sharing first places equally with team-mate Prost.*

Generally regarded as one of the most remarkable new talents to explode upon the Formula 1 scene in the last five years, Ayrton Senna's meteoric racing career can be said to have begun when he stepped into a home-made kart at the age of four! By the time he was 13, he had notched up his first official kart victory in his native Brazil. Even at this early stage of his career, Ayrton was attracting attention as an unusually committed and determined young man.

Born Ayrton Senna da Silva on 21 March 1960

in São Paulo, he won the South American Kart championship in 1977–80, and in 1981 moved to England to contest his first full season of Formula Ford 1600. The ease with which he swept his rivals aside to win the RAC and Townsend Thoresen titles was hugely impressive, and the margins by which he triumphed in FF2000 events the following year were so astonishing that even some F1 team managers began to take notice.

At the end of the 1982 season he won his maiden F3 race at Thruxton before returning to Brazil to line up sponsorship to enable him to take part in a complete British F3 programme the following year.

In a closely fought campaign Senna eventually edged out home boy Martin Brundle to take the title, mixing superb natural balance and car control with a self-confidence uncanny in one so young.

The Toleman team quickly snapped him up for Formula 1 in 1984 and he scored his first championship point on his second outing, in South Africa. From that point onwards his learning curve shot skywards. At Monaco, in the streaming rain, he had all but caught Prost (and had made the fastest lap) when the race was stopped prematurely; and he rounded off the year with a terrific third place behind the McLaren–TAGs in the Portuguese Grand Prix at Estoril at a time when Alain Prost and Niki Lauda were virtually toying with the opposition during their successful inter-team battle for the championship. Senna and Mansell both notched 13 points that season.

After making a somewhat awkward departure from Toleman, Senna switched to Lotus for 1985 and found a winning car beneath him for the first time. He won his second race for the team in pouring rain at Estoril, and later took the Belgian Grand Prix at Spa. Still using a Renault engine, Lotus swept him on for another couple of victories in 1986. The index of a grand-prix driver's true talent is how he performs in the wet. In that second place at Monaco in 1984 and with the Estoril win in 1985, Senna established his F1 credentials in truly brilliant fashion.

In 1987, the Lotus-Honda package didn't match up to Senna's high hopes, so the Brazilian perfectionist quickly did a deal with Honda Marlboro–McLaren to run alongside Alain Prost in 1988. After four years learning his F1 trade, Senna now matches up to the acknowledged best in the world at the wheel of equal machinery. It will be his ultimate test. The committed and super-sensitive test driver now has the opportunity to establish himself as the most outstanding talent of all in the grand prix game. All he has to do is beat Prost, a task he clearly feels confident about.

PRACTICE

Below The Williams
pit during practice
sessions before the
1986 Mexican Grand
Prix. If two spare cars
are available, one is
allocated to each
driver and is set up in
exactly the same way
as his race car.

By the time a grand-prix race begins, the competing drivers know the circuit inside out. They have made mental notes of, say, a dubious strip of kerbing on the inside apex of a certain corner and where a patch of re-surfacing has made the circuit particularly slippery; worked out the best places to try out overtaking manoeuvres; and have learned how their car will perform in the early stages of the race when the fuel tank is full and the tyres not fully warmed up. They will have assimilated this information during the two days of official practice which precedes every grand-prix on the calendar.

To the outside observer, F1 practice and quali-

fying look like total chaos. Some cars seem forever trapped in the pit lane, apparently appearing only for the odd two- or three-lap sprint, while others seem to be lapping the circuit all the time. The reality of the situation is that every team is operating to a carefully worked-out plan of action, hopefully ending up with its cars on the front row of the starting grid for Sunday's race.

In recent years, practice and qualifying have evolved into a standard format. On the Friday and Saturday before the race (Thursday and Saturday at Monaco) there is an untimed session, which does not count for grid positions, each

Left A Goodyear
engineer checks the
temperature of
Mansell's front tyres.
Each grand-prix
circuit has a different
effect on tyres in
terms of wear and
running temperature,
and different tyre
compounds are tried
in the search for
optimum
performance.

morning from 10.00 to 11.30. Then there is an hour of official qualifying from 13.00 to 14.00. Finally, on race morning, there is a half-hour warm-up session just to make final checks and adjustments prior to the start of the grand prix.

Since the start of the 1987 season Goodyear has had a tyre-supply monopoly in Formula 1, and each team is allotted eight sets of tyres per car per race. Only two of these sets can be used by each car during the timed qualifying sessions. This regulation was originally introduced to prevent teams using an unlimited number of super-sticky qualifying tyres in the days when Goodyear, Michelin and Pirelli were all battling for victory in the F1 arena. With Goodyear assuming the task of supplying all the teams, qualifying tyres were no longer produced, but the limit of two sets per car per session was retained. And to make sure nobody cheats, those two nominated sets per car are painted with the stencilled car's race number on their sidewalls. Each time the car leaves the pit lane it must pass four marshals who check that it is using tyres marked with the correct number.

A team may well have availed itself of some pre-race testing at a given circuit prior to race weekend but, in general, that will have provided only a broad base of information: changes of temperature, or even such an apparently minor matter as a change in the wind, can affect a car's performance 'on the day'. And of course the surface of each circuit is different from all the others in a variety of ways.

The first unofficial session sees most teams 'limbering up' in preparation for the serious business of the afternoon. There may be a new gearbox which needs running in, or a minor change of suspension geometry which has been fitted to the spare car so that a driver can assess whether it is an improvement over the set-up on his race car. This 'back to back' testing often provides an invaluable short-cut to improved

Left *Changing the ratios of the gears on a Ferrari F187 during the first unofficial practice session for the 1987 Monaco Grand Prix. Each F1 circuit requires a different combination of gears; the slow, many-cornered Monaco circuit calls for lower gearing than the faster tracks such as the Österreichring and Silverstone.*

Right Michele Alboreto (Ferrari F186) confers with his pit team during practice for the 1986 San Marino Grand Prix. Fifth fastest qualifier, Alboreto was denied fourth place in the race by turbocharger failure, Ferrari's greatest bugbear during the 1986 championship.

performance and is carried out by virtually every team that can afford to have a spare car on hand for the weekend.

There is also the question of sizing up the opposition. It may be that one of the teams has made some sort of technical break-through since the last race. The untimed Friday morning session can be useful to the other teams in assessing the effects of that improvement. Of course, the team in question may play a cautious game, unwilling to show their hand before the second timed qualifying session on Saturday afternoon. One of the fascinations of the practice sessions for experienced observers of the sport lies in detecting the gamesmanship indulged in by the various teams.

By the end of the first 90-minute session, the drivers will be getting into the swing of things and running quite quickly. But they may well have decided that they need a change of gear ratios before the first qualifying session; or perhaps an engine has lost a few revs at high speed, suggesting that it is in need of replacement. So the lunchbox between the two sessions is anything but restful for the mechanics. While they slave away changing gear ratios, springs and ride heights, the driver will probably be in deep discussion with the engineers and, possibly, the designer. Should they leave that engine in for first qualifying and change it tonight? Is the spare car ready in case they have a failure? Perhaps they could move the steering wheel a little closer? Is there any way in which they could move the brake-balance control down a bit in the cockpit? – the driver might be grazing it with his knuckle when he locks over into a hairpin. So the complaints, debates and discussions go on.

QUALIFYING LAPS

If everything is running well, the top teams will be seen moving at least one of their cars down the pit lane about 10 minutes before the start of first qualifying. The driver, helmet and gloves already on, will sit motionless in the cockpit waiting for the track to open. These teams have decided to 'go early'. That is to say, their drivers will attempt

Below An engineer makes an adjustment to the suspension of a 1986 Arrows-BMW A8. As with the selection of gearbox ratios, fine tuning of a car's suspension for a particular circuit depends greatly on the reports of the driver during practice sessions.

Above Ayrton Senna (Lotus-Honda) in the 1987 Brazilian Grand Prix, the first F1 race of the season. With a new engine (albeit one race-developed by Williams) and radically new suspension, Lotus's practice sessions before the race were scrutinized even more carefully than usual by their rivals.

to capitalise on a relatively traffic-free circuit to get a fast qualifying lap under their belt before too many other cars are out there to get in the way. Once this has been achieved, they often retire to the pits and watch, hawk-like, to see who goes quicker before they make their second run. Each team is connected up to the official electronic timing system which records the lap times during qualifying – and during the race itself – so each team knows what the others are doing.

Farther back down the pit lane you may see a driver such as Ayrton Senna take his helmet off after a quick, early run and loll against the pit wall as if he hasn't a care in the world. But don't be fooled into thinking that he is not watching. The chances are that he will be monitoring every rival's move with eagle-eyed accuracy and, when he walks casually back across the pit lane to his car, you just *know* that something spectacular is about to happen. Senna is one of those inspired performers who can extract the ultimate from a grand-prix car in any given situation. But watching him prepare for a really quick qualifying lap is like watching as an orchestra works itself up to a controlled frenzy for the spectacular finale of a symphony.

To start with, the pace seems gentle, almost casual. But if you watch closely, you will see that the team is a disciplined, skilfully interlocking group of like-minded individuals. Senna will have made a mental note of where all his rivals are on the circuit: 'Prost has done his two runs, so no need to worry about him; Mansell's race car stopped out on the circuit, so he's using the spare – which seems to be in the pits with gearbox trouble; the Ferraris . . . yes, I can deal with them. That leaves the quick Brabham and two Benettons. Right, I'll go now. . . .'

One mechanic will have pumped fuel out of the spare Lotus, which has now been set up in

Right A nap-hand of 1987 Honda engines in the Lotus pit. Spare engines are essential because even two units meticulously prepared by the same engineers may reveal quite different characteristics during practice sessions.

'qualifying' specification: it needs only the bare minimum of fuel for a three-lap run; it is fitted with weight-saving carbon-fibre brake discs; the turbo boost pressure will be turned up as high as it can be without 'tripping' the mandatory boost-control valve. Now Senna climbs aboard. His belts are tightened. And he's away. . . .

Remember, he has only a few laps before the tyres begin to lose the fine edge of their grip, so he needs to grab as traffic-free a lap as possible while he still has maximum adhesion. That can some-times be difficult. Senna and his rivals must balance risk against realism: he must judge expertly whether he can overtake a certain car going into a certain tricky corner, while relying on his rival's judgement not to move over on him.

Suddenly, Senna is on his fastest lap. The air is almost alive with excitement as he slams round the circuit, trips the timing beam and eases off the throttle. Just as suddenly it is all over. Maybe he has set the fastest time; perhaps only second fastest. Word comes down the pit lane: 'Prost is fastest'. The World Champion's rivals shake their heads. English driver Martin Brundle shrugs: 'You know, in my three years of Formula 1, I have *never* seen Prost on what looked like a qualifying lap. He's just so smooth nobody's ever aware he is going quickly. Or do they just give him pole position as a matter of course?' Every-body laughs – but in 1986 it was Senna who was the undoubted pole 'king'.

At 14.00 on Friday it is all over until tomorrow. Cars are pushed back into their pit garages and drivers disappear with their team managers into motorhomes to 'de-brief'. This means they go through the day's work in lap-by-lap detail, probing each other's thoughts, analysing the times, speculating where time might be lost or gained. Meanwhile, the mechanics are maybe taking a few minutes off for a well-earned sandwich and a drink. But their work could well go on for several hours more.

After an hour or two, the engineers emerge from the de-brief and confer with the chief mechanics. A job list is produced to cover all the changes that need to be made to the team's cars before Saturday practice begins. These can range from routine, if lengthy, tasks such as an engine or gearbox change, to more complex work. Perhaps one engine has a mysterious misfire which has proved impossible to cure. There may be a

Left *Senna checks the lap times of his rivals before putting in a qualifying lap on the second practice day. The VDU shows a read-out from the official electronic timing system which* records lap times during both qualifying and the race proper.

Above *Alain Prost and Keke Rosberg at a debriefing session during qualifying for the 1986 Monaco Grand Prix. White-shirted McLaren team manager Ron Dennis is behind* Prost, who later drove brilliantly to take first place in the race, Rosberg following him home to take second place – his best result of the season.

problem in its electrical circuits, so it may have to be totally stripped.

Another car may have a tricky fuel-system problem – perhaps the fuel pump just will not pick up the last few gallons when the fuel load goes down. That really is a major drama, because with only 195 litres (about 43 gallons) of fuel permitted by the regulations, every eggcupful counts in the race. The problem must be rectified in time for Saturday practice, so the whole fuel cell may have to be changed. That is a long job.

In addition, there is routine maintenance to be carried out. Suspension components have to be checked, all the cockpit instruments are looked over. The electrical system will be examined by mechanics with the patience and care of a surgeon carrying out a delicate operation.

PRACTICE: DAY TWO

Come Saturday morning and it's as though Friday never happened. With that sense of unquenchable optimism which you need to survive in as demanding a world as grand-prix racing, everybody is up early and raring to go. The previous day's trials and tribulations are being swept to the back of everybody's minds. Saturday's untimed morning session almost certainly sees many cars running with full fuel loads. This enables the teams to get some idea of what sort of fuel-consumption figures they can expect for the following day's race. It also helps decide what gear ratios to use and, also, how best to set up the car's ride height.

A racing-car's gearbox bears little resemblance to that in a family saloon. Most top teams use six-speed gearboxes which are specially designed and built for the individual car in which they are used. More importantly, the gear ratios can be changed in an hour or so in order to get the very best performance out of an engine on any given circuit. The demands of a gruelling street circuit such as Monaco or Detroit, for instance, are quite different from those of the ultra-fast tracks such as the Österreichring or Silverstone.

On tight circuits, low gears are fitted to produce

Right McLaren engineers working on the MP4/3, the 1987 version of the TAG engine. By mid-season, the Williams-Honda was clearly the fastest car on the F1 circuits, only the McLaren's chassis and Prost's superlative skills keeping his team in contention.

the best acceleration out of tight corners. The hill up to Casino Square at Monaco is steep (about 1 in 8) and the cars need as much 'punch' as possible to sprint up to the top in double-quick time. Maximum speed is of less importance than on a really fast circuit where high gears are fitted to the cars, enabling them to accelerate smoothly in fifth and sixth gears towards their maximum potential speed without over-revving the engine. A car with a top gear suitable for the 150mph dash through the curving tunnel at Monaco would be over-revving madly if asked to do 190mph at Silverstone. That would not only risk damaging the engine but, just as important, ruin its fuel-consumption figures, so that it could well run out of fuel before the end of the race. It might be thought that, with six gears at his disposal, a designer could produce a gearbox suitable for all circuits. But sports cars of every kind, and racing-cars especially, need what is called a close-ratio box, in which the ratio of one gear does not differ greatly from those of the gears immediately below and above it. Such a box, given slick gear-changing, provides better acceleration than one whose gear ratios are widely spaced.

Even a change in the wind can affect the car's performance and require subtle adjustment of the gears. In Saturday's untimed session there may be a headwind on the main straight. On the face of it, that means a lower sixth gear in order that the car can 'pull' harder against the gale. But, if such a change is made during the lunch break, that car could well find itself over-revving if the head wind changes to a tail wind before qualifying starts!

All these considerations have to be taken into account and a compromise reached. Similarly, deciding on the car's optimum ride height can be fraught with difficulty. 'Ride height' is the crucial gap between the underside of the car and the surface of the track; in the interests of good

Left *Peter Wright and Lotus colleagues running a computer test on Senna's suspension. On today's F1 cars, ride height (the gap between the car's underside and the road) is crucial to the car's handling and aerodynamics. With a full tank of fuel, the ride height may be less than one inch. The new 'active-ride' suspension maintains constant ride height under all loads.*

roadholding, handling, and aerodynamic efficiency, the gap must be as small and as unvarying as possible.

Of course, if a car is set up with its ride height at 1½ inches with a full fuel load aboard, this may well increase to two inches once the fuel load is consumed and the car becomes lighter. So another compromise is required. With a full load of fuel aboard, the car may well be set up with a ride height of only half an inch. That guarantees that, as the fuel load lightens, the car will rise slightly to somewhere near its optimum ride height. During practice and qualifying and the early stages of a race, you can always tell the cars that are running with a full fuel load by the trail of sparks as they 'bottom out', their undersides hitting the track whenever they go over a bump. Recent developments have centred on 'active-ride' computer-controlled suspension to maintain a constant ride height. In 1987 Lotus were early leaders in this department.

The final Saturday qualifying session turns into a far more frenzied affair than that on the previous afternoon. For those drivers who had technical trouble on Friday, this is their last chance to improve their qualifying time. Again, only two marked sets of tyres per car are permitted, and this rule is strenuously enforced. It is permissible for a driver to do two runs and then go out again on a mixed set of tyres, the best used pair from each of his previous two sets, but no more than eight tyres per car must be used. If a driver should be unfortunate enough to suffer a puncture, that is his misfortune. No replacement tyres are allowed.

POLE POSITION

The objective of all this effort is to qualify for 'pole' position – that is, the number one starting position on the grid. The cars line up for the grand prix start in pairs, the faster of each pair 'staggered' slightly ahead of the other. Pole position is thus slightly forward of the second place qualifier on the opposite side of the track.

The benefits are innumerable. The most obvious empty track ahead of him. If he makes a good

Right Last-minute checks to Nelson Piquet's Williams-Honda FW11 before he sets out on a final qualifying lap. The front and rear aerofoils, side pods and cramped cockpit are typical of all present-day F1 cars. Note also the slick (treadless) tyres.

advantage is that the pole-position man has an start and can sustain the pace, he has a good chance of leading throughout, especially on city-street circuits where it is very difficult to over-take. Second, the pole-position man usually starts on the side of the track offering the best possible line through the first corner. This will not necessarily be the best line when he is racing hard and approaching the corner at speed; but from a standing start he will arrive at the corner more slowly, and he may well be able to snatch an early advantage.

Prestige, of course, has its part to play. There is a psychological advantage in starting from pole position which, in some cases, has a driver's rivals beaten almost before the start. But it is not a position without its responsibilities.

Before the start, there is a formation (or parade) lap away from the grid. The cars return, line-up, and are then unleashed by the green starting light. The pole-position man is the one from whom everybody else takes their lead. He must lead them round the parade lap not too quickly, and not too slowly. Running too quickly may heap problems on himself. If he arrives back on pole position too soon, he may have to sit waiting with the engine running for longer than is ideal. That might result in the first signs of engine overheating; it also uses up precious fuel.

On the other hand, if he goes too slowly, the pack behind will crowd in on him, become edgy and over-anxious and, as a result, perhaps get away at the green light to a ragged start which can cause all sorts of problems from banging wheels to a multiple pile-up.

The routine after second qualifying is much the same as the previous afternoon. The drivers emerge from the debriefs either elated or de-

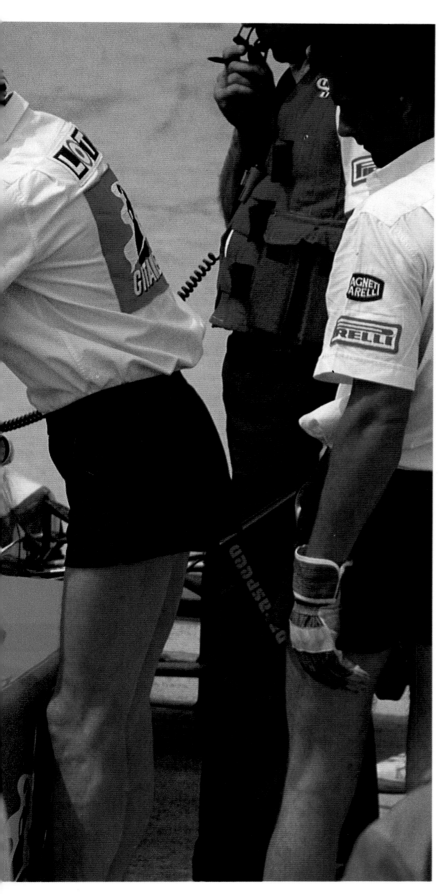

Left Fuelling up René Arnoux's Ligier-Renault JS27 before the start of the 1986 Hungarian Grand Prix. The fuelling is carefully monitored by race officials. Arnoux's team-mate Philippe Alliot, replacing Jacques Laffite (injured in the British Grand Prix), took a creditable ninth place at Budapest.

pressed, depending on their qualifying positions, and comments to the mechanics range from 'I want this, that and something else changed' to 'Please don't touch it. It's absolutely perfect!'

The fastest 26 cars start the race, except at Monaco where the field is usually restricted to 20. If more have taken part in practice, that's bad luck. The 27th competitor, however, always takes part in the race-morning warm-up, just in case something happens to one of the other competitors.

Saturday night is the toughest for the mechanics. Many teams change the engine on all their cars, using the new ones for the following day's race and then during qualifying for the next grand prix on the calendar. All the knowledge and experience gained during the two previous days is considered, distilled in the engineers' minds and then minutely analysed yet again. After this deliberation is complete, the final detailed set-up for the car will be specified.

On race morning, the half-hour warm-up session is usually the most reliable indicator of form in the race to follow. All the cars will be running in race trim, with no qualifying 'tweaks'. Suddenly it may become apparent that Prost, who has perhaps only qualified fourth on the grid, is easily the quickest. He could be the man to watch when it comes to the serious business of the weekend.

These race-morning sessions are not without their dramas. An engine failure now produces what, to the outsider, looks like acute panic. Mechanics fall on the car and begin a lightning engine change to prepare the car for the race. It may look like a circus but, in fact, most teams work to a prescribed routine in such circumstances. They work fast, but with great accuracy.

Finally the moment arrives. The cars are fuelled up and wheeled out to the starting grid. That two days of frantic activity is over. All that remains is the 200 mile sprint to the chequered flag.

By the end of the afternoon, some will be elated, others dejected. Either way, they will be back at another circuit two weeks later, starting all over again with the same glimmer of optimism in their eye. This time, surely, it will be different!

Right The 26 qualifying cars line up on the starting grid at Imola for the 1987 San Marino Grand Prix. Senna is in pole position – he had also taken pole in eight of the 16 races in 1986, including San Marino. Nigel Mansell and Alain Prost are next on the grid.

FOUR TO WATCH

Gerhard Berger

At the end of the 1985 season, after a year with the Arrows team, it was by no means certain that Gerhard Berger would be staying in grand-prix racing the following year. Unquestionably, he had the talent and ability. But in such a high-powered world, sponsorship considerations do not always take such factors into account.

Happily, the genial 27 year old from Worgl, near Innsbruck, found a vacant niche in the Benetton-BMW squad. Less than 12 months later he was standing on the victory rostrum at Mexico City, having just scored the team's maiden grand-prix success. And six weeks after that he had signed to drive for the most famous team in the business – Ferrari.

By any standards, Berger's progress through the motor-racing ranks has been meteoric. He first sprang to prominence in the European Alfasud championship, finishing seventh in the contest at his first attempt. Formula 3 followed in 1983 with Gerhard quickly demonstrating considerable promise and prowess in this hotly contested category. Although he did not win one of the European Championship rounds, he did manage a couple of second places to finish joint seventh in the points table, equal with Martin Brundle.

Berger then tackled the European Touring Car Championship, where his spectacular form at the wheel of the BMW 635 coupés attracted the attention of the ATS Formula 1 team. He drove for them in the 1984 Austrian Grand Prix and, although he failed to finish at Zeltweg, a few weeks later he stormed home an impressive sixth in the Italian Grand Prix at Monza. (The fact that he was not originally registered as one of the season's regular F1 contestants precluded his being awarded the single point which goes to the driver taking sixth place.)

It seemed that new vistas of opportunity were opening up for Gerhard, but his racing career very nearly ended when he was involved in a serious road accident near his home in Austria shortly after the end of the season. Fortunate to escape with fractured vertebrae in his neck, he spent most of the winter recuperating. But he was well enough to join Thierry Boutsen in the Arrows-BMW squad at the start of the 1985 Championship season and rounded off that year with a fifth place in South Africa and sixth in Australia.

In 1986 he really began to mature, handling the Benetton-BMW with such flair and expertise that it was easy to forget he had less than two seasons' F1 experience. He led his home grand prix commandingly at the Österreichring until he was forced into the pits with battery problems; but he judged things superbly in the searing heat of Mexico to win that country's grand prix, thanks to a non-stop run on Pirelli rubber – when all his Goodyear-shod rivals were having to stop two or even three times.

After a shaky start with Ferrari, Gerhard steadily picked up the pace and asserted his quality as a front-runner from the middle of the 1987 season, consistently outpacing his teammate Michele Alboreto. Finally, at Suzuka, he won the Japanese Grand Prix to return the Prancing Horse to the winner's circle for the first time in over two years. He followed that up a fortnight later with a blisteringly dominant victory in the Australian GP at Adelaide, and he faced 1988 as the strongest contender for the World Championship outside McLaren, Williams and Lotus.

Below left *Gerhard Berger joined Michele Alboreto in the Italian équipe for 1987. He replaced Stefan Johansson who became Prost's partner at McLaren-TAG in succession to Keke Rosberg.*

Below *Berger in the Ferrari F187 at the 1987 Brazilian Grand Prix, where he came in fourth. The car, designed by Gustav Brunner, had some finishing touches from John Barnard's R and D facility in Britain.*

Alessandro Nannini

Two years of struggling with the uncompetitive Minardi have finally brought Alessandro Nannini his long overdue reward with a place in the 1988 Benetton-Ford line-up alongside Thierry Boutsen. In truth, the way he doggedly had pushed the unwieldy Minardi much further up the starting grids than it deserved had served to underline that this 28-year-old from Siena was cut out for better things.

Nannini's competition career began behind the wheel of a most unlikely machine – a Citroën Dyane. Rather than follow what might be described as the 'conventional route' into karting, Alessandro went rallying with his Citroën and quickly graduated to the cockpit of a Lancia Stratos, the F1 car of the rally world throughout much of the 1970s.

In 1980 he turned to circuit racing with a single-seater Formula Fiat Abarth, winning on only his third outing. In 1981 he triumphed in the Italian national championship before moving directly into Formula 2 with Minardi at the start of 1982. He was fifth in his first race, at Silverstone, and wound up a promising tenth overall in the European Championship series.

Unfortunately, he was beset by mechanical unreliability throughout 1983 and 1984, but kept his reputation afloat with some splendid outings at the wheel of the works Lancia sports cars in endurance events. In 1984 he and co-driver Bob Wollek qualified on pole position at Le Mans and Alessandro established a new circuit record before his retirement.

Plans to graduate to F1 in 1985 were thwarted when the sport's governing body, FISA, felt he had insufficient results in F2 to warrant awarding him a super licence; so he spent what was a fourth year driving for Lancia and wound up getting the appropriate licence at the start of 1986.

He drove for Minardi throughout 1986 and 1987, but never managed a finish in the Championship points owing to the car's poor record of reliability. His move to Benetton should improve his prospects considerably, although he wryly admits that it is unlikely he will ever be recognised in his native land as the most famous member of the Nannini family: his sister Gianna is one of Italy's top rock singers!

Main picture *The 1988 Benetton-Ford B188 piloted by Alessandro Nannini. The équipe exchanged its 1987 turbocharged Ford Cosworth engine for a normally aspirated, 3.5-litre Cosworth DFR.*

Inset *After coaxing non-competitive hardware around the F1 circuits for two years, the gifted Nannini joined Thierry Boutsen in a promising partnership with a small but ambitious team.*

Below Thierry Boutsen's mount for 1987 — the Rory Byrne-designed Benetton B187, powered by the V6 Ford-Cosworth turbocharged engine. One of the most impressive-looking cars on the circuit in 1987, the B187 had still to establish itself as truly competitive against the might of the Williams, Lotus, and McLaren teams.

Right Boutsen, having spent three years with the Arrows team variously partnering Berger, Marc Surer and Christian Danner, leapt at Peter Collins' invitation to drive for Benetton after Berger's departure to Ferrari.

Thierry Boutsen

There is something about Thierry Boutsen that exudes star quality in abundance. He is a good-natured 30-year-old with impeccable manners and a gentle demeanour. But out on the track he is absolutely uncompromising in battle, while retaining an immaculate driving style.

Attracted to the sport by the exploits of fellow Belgian Jacky Ickx, Boutsen's first real taste of the business came when he attended the racing drivers' school at Zolder at the age of 18. By 1977 he had managed to buy his own car, an elderly Formula Ford Hawke, but it was not until 1978 that he really began to make his mark. At the wheel of a Crossle, he won 15 out of the 18 races he contested, clinching the Benelux Championship before moving into Formula 3 in 1979.

In 1980 he finished second behind Michele Alboreto in the European F3 Championship at the wheel of a Martini. From there his career progressed into Formula 2 in 1981, when he won a couple of races in a March-BMW before joining the Spirit-Honda team the following year.

When Honda nominated the Spirit team to try out its prototype turbocharged grand-prix engine in 1983, Boutsen hoped he would be the one nominated to race it. He was to be disappointed, that privilege falling to Stefan Johansson. Undaunted, he raised sufficient sponsorship to clinch a contract with the Arrows team, for which he first raced in the 1983 Belgian GP at Spa.

The limitations of his machinery kept Boutsen's talent largely concealed over the next three seasons, although it was there for the experts to see if they really looked. The superb way he held down fourth place at Spa in 1985 until his machine wilted with mechanical failure a couple of laps from the finish gave undeniable evidence of his true ability and potential. Boutsen also excelled at the wheel of Porsche sportscars and his victory over the works Jaguars in the Spa endurance race at the end of 1986 helped sustain his reputation on the F1 driver market.

Benetton team manager Peter Collins had never doubted Boutsen's talent so, when he became available at the end of his Arrows contract, he was quickly snapped up to fill the slot left vacant by Berger's switch to Ferrari at the start of 1987.

The 1987 season proved disappointing for Boutsen whose Benetton-Ford B187 turbo simply did not prove reliable enough for him to unlock his great talent. Time and again the Ford-engined cars ran with the leading bunch only to be let down by silly mechanical problems. At Mexico, for the first time in his career, he led commandingly, but it didn't last. This genial Belgian with the calm and even temperament will be hoping for better things now the team has switched to naturally aspirated engines in 1988.

Jonathan Palmer

Known affectionately amongst his peers as 'the Doc', Jonathan Palmer's level-headed attitude towards motor-racing is reflected by the fact that he completed his medical training and qualified as a doctor before tackling a full-time career in professional motor racing. Born in 1957, he qualified in 1979 and held two hospital posts before relinquishing his medical career.

He had originally been introduced to the sport through his father, Dr Jack Palmer, who had been Chief Medical Officer for the British Automobile Racing Club. Jonathan began racing with an Austin-Healey sports car in 1975 before switching to Formula Ford. In 1981 he won one of the coveted Grovewood Awards, presented to young British drivers who show outstanding promise, and then set himself firmly on the path to international recognition by clinching the 1982 British Formula 3 Championship in fine style. In 1982 he moved up into F2, won the European Championship the following year, and made his grand-prix debut in the third Williams in the 1983 Brands Hatch Grand Prix of Europe.

In 1984 he signed for the RAM team for his first full F1 season, switching to Zakspeed for 1985 and 1986. Both were relatively small and moderately-financed teams, with little more racing experience in the top league than Jonathan himself. None the less, 'the Doc' proved himself a cool, methodical racer whose orderly mind and clear-sighted approach helped him gain a reputation as a test and development driver.

Palmer's first full F1 season was interspersed with a successful programme of sportscar racing for the privately fielded, British-based Richard Lloyd Porsche team in the World Sportscar Championship. At the end of 1986 he took a gamble. Anxious to promote his career at the highest possible level, he held out on the off-chance that he might be offered the second McLaren drive alongside Alain Prost. Sadly, it was a vain hope: the drive went to Stefan Johansson. Meanwhile, fellow Englishman Martin Brundle had been signed up as his replacement at Zakspeed, briefly leaving Palmer out in the wilderness until his career was rescued by the chance to drive for Ken Tyrrell.

The 1987 season proved to be the making of Jonathan Palmer, the Tyrrell DG/016 allowing him to display superb form against the odds, notably at Monaco where he balanced speed and skill to bring his mount home fifth – the best GP placing of his career to date. One of the best balanced individuals in the F1 business, Palmer should have a better than even chance of running in the front half of the field in 1988. Privately, he considers it realistic to think in terms of his first grand prix victory. . . .

Above Jonathan Palmer in 1987 Tyrrell strip. He and Brundle swapped équipes at the end of 1986 after Palmer had proved himself a gifted test and development driver in his two seasons with the Zakspeed team.

Right Palmer driving the Tyrrell-Ford DG016 in the 1987 Brazilian Grand Prix. Later, at Monaco, he drove a fine race to earn his first-ever championship points.

IN THE PITS

Watching the action on a television screen, you might well be forgiven for concluding that the average Formula 1 pit lane is nothing more than a disorganised jumble of men and machines. In fact, nothing could be further from the truth. Crowded it may well be on race day, but beneath that appearance of terminal frenzy everything is planned out with meticulous care and carried out with military precision.

The pit lane is the operational heart of the grand prix, functioning in much the same way as, for example, a military airfield controls its fighter planes. It is in the pit lane garages that the cars are prepared before a day's practice or racing, and it is to those garages that they return at the end of the action. All the time, they are tended by and worried over by a squad of highly trained and single-minded mechanics.

In the past few years the sport's governing body, FISA, has laid down stringent pit specifications which must be adhered to by circuits wishing to stage world championship-qualifying grands prix. But if we go back 20 years or so, the life of a Formula 1 mechanic was gruelling, to say the least. Criss-crossing Europe before the current motorway network was anything like complete, the mechanics travelled cramped into often old, slow and unreliable transporters. When it came to preparing the cars at the circuits, the work was often carried out in the open, irrespective of whether it was hot or cold, wet or dry. Engine, gearbox and suspension components could be seen scattered over the paddock surface around the car. If they were lucky, the mechanics might get a sandwich and a cup of coffee before their toil ended at around midnight.

How different things are today. Top grand-prix teams move their cars and equipment round Europe in luxurious, purpose-built transporters which are designed and equipped with all the attention to detail that goes into the manufacture of the Formula 1 cars they contain. There will be a couple of men employed solely to drive the trucks and generally help with stowing equipment, while the mechanics fly in on specially organised charter flights the day before first practice, and fly out again the night after the race. That way they can be back home and perhaps enjoy a well-earned day off on the Monday after a race before the transporter

Below *First day at the new circuit: world champion Alain Prost and his McLaren-TAG MP4/2C take a photocall, in August 1986, before the practice sessions at the Hungaroring for the first Hungarian Grand Prix since World War II. Drivers had to get to know every foot of the unfamiliar circuit as well as helping to put their cars into competitive trim for the race.*

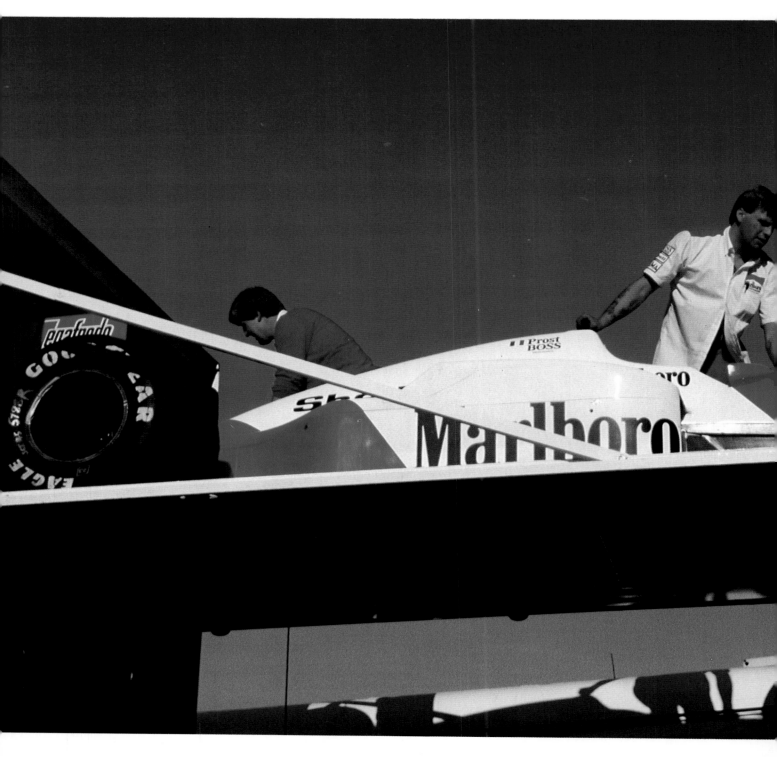

Above Alain Prost's
McLaren-TAG on the
tail lift of the team's
transporter. The cars
and equipment, and
pit teams travel to and
from circuits all over
Europe in their vast
trucks.

arrives back at base on the Tuesday and preparation begins for the next race on the schedule.

PRACTICE DAYS

With Formula 1 practice and qualifying taking place on the Friday and Saturday prior to a grand prix, the transporters roll into the paddock on the Wednesday or Thursday. Before the cars can be readied for practice there is an enormous amount of hard work and detailed preparation to carry out, starting from the moment the transporter's huge rear doors drop down and the cars are rolled out into the pit lane garages.

The mechanics work as a well-drilled team. Top teams will have three men assigned to each car (the two nominated race cars and the spare). There will also be a gearbox specialist, technicians from the engine builder/supplier, an electrical expert, and a tyre fitter. While the cars are being unpacked with loving care, the tyre fitter will be taking the team's wheel rims to the tyre-supply truck to be fitted with the most suitable tyre for the job at that particular circuit.

Each mechanic has his own selection of tools: purpose-built trolleys, with all the tools on display, are wheeled to the front of the pit lane garage. Whatever tool is needed in a sudden mid-race crisis can be found in an instant.

Supplies of fuel are also kept at the back of the pit; air lines are connected to the high-speed

Right *Alain Prost, team boss Ron Dennis (rear, left) and other McLaren team members confer in the transporter during practice sessions at Estoril for the 1986 Portuguese GP.*

power sockets for tightening or unscrewing the wheel-securing nuts. Inside the transporter a complete range of spares and accessories for each car is carried in purpose-built compartments; and once the cars have been unloaded, workbenches and power tools are available to create a self-contained mobile workshop capable of dealing with most technical disasters – short of a total write-off – during the grand-prix weekend.

On Friday morning the mechanics arrive early to complete the final detailed preparation of each car prior to the start of the first untimed practice session. By 8.00 am, two hours before the action begins, the cars will probably be ready, but right up to the moment they are rolled out on to the grid the mechanics will be fussing over them. If the weather is cold, radiator intakes will have been taped over so that the oil and water come up to working temperature as quickly as possible once the car starts running. If new brake pads, or perhaps a new gearbox, have been fitted the previous night, a note will be taped to the centre of the steering wheel, reminding the driver to take things carefully for the first few laps.

Then, of course, there are the spare parts: not only wheels and tyres, but spare wings, and a selection of nose sections painted with the correct race numbers. In an emergency, everybody knows what to do in a flash. Life in the pits may look fairly casual during untimed practice, but if quick action is needed – to change damaged bodywork, or to fit a new rear wing or a fresh set of tyres a few minutes before the end of the qualifying period, the mechanics spring into action with electrifying efficiency.

On the Saturday night before the race most teams will strip down their cars completely and fit freshly rebuilt engines. Then, on the Sunday morning, the relentless countdown to the race begins. There is an almost palpable tension among the mechanics as the cars edge out on to the track for the half-hour warm-up session. If

Right Practice days in the pits: two engineers from the Honda factory at work on the engine of Nelson Piquet's 1986 Williams-Honda FW11 in preparation for qualifying sessions for the Italian Grand Prix at Monza. Honda-engined cars proved to be comfortably the fastest here, Piquet and Mansell taking first and second places in the race.

there is a major problem now, things will be tight: an engine failure at this late stage can be a major drama. A well-drilled team could change an engine in the time available, but it would be a mammoth undertaking. If it has to be done, the mechanics from all three cars will muck in together to complete the task as quickly and efficiently as possible. Meanwhile, the spare car will be receiving an extra polish, its fuel tank topped up and a set of race tyres fitted – just in case it's going to be needed.

As the cars line up on the grid, the mechanics tending the spare car can afford to relax a bit. It looks as though their car can now be pushed back to the garage, pumped dry of its fuel load and prepared for loading into the transporter. But even when the red light gives way to the green and the pack is sprinting towards the first corner, their work may not be over. In the 1986 British Grand Prix, a multiple pile-up on the first corner resulted in the race being red-flagged to a halt after only one lap. By this time, Nigel Mansell's Williams had suffered a driveshaft breakage and was coasting slowly at the back of the field, the Englishman believing his chances to be over. Stopping and restarting the race gave him a tremendous second chance. However, there was no way in which the driveshaft could be changed in the time available, so the Williams mechanics rolled out the spare car to take its place, confident in the knowledge it was fully race-worthy in every respect. Mansell happily changed cars – and went on to score a momentous victory in front of a delighted home crowd.

Below *Ayrton Senna's Lotus-Honda having its one-piece body panel lowered into position in the pits before the 1987 San Marino Grand Prix at Imola.*

Left *Nigel Mansell in a last-minute conference before a 1986 practice session.*

THE RACE

During a race, it is best to keep away from the pits unless your presence is absolutely essential. The pit lane is part of the racing circuit and, in these days of routine pit stops to change tyres, racing cars usually enter it at racing speeds.

Two laps or so before a car is going to make a tyre stop, the mechanics are ready and waiting. They will have already laid a distinctive trail of coloured tape right up to the exact point in the pit lane where the car is to stop. At the back of the pit garages the replacement tyres are being heated in their tailor-made 'electric blankets'. Tyres naturally generate considerable heat in a race, so the manufacturers make tyres that operate most efficiently at racing temperature. The blankets heat the tyres to the required temperature, so that the driver does not have to waste time warming them up on the circuit. From the pit exit, or at least within a few hundred yards of it, he should be able to 'lean' on his tyres as hard as he likes!

Suddenly the moment has arrived! 'Their man' – Prost, Piquet, Mansell, Senna or whoever – hurtles into the pit lane and brakes to a halt, perfectly in position. The air is split with the metallic whirring of the wheel-locking sockets. Old wheels off: new wheels on: more whirring. The chief mechanic, standing at the front of the car facing the driver, waits until his colleagues at all four corners signify they have finished their task by leaping upright and raising one hand above the head. Then the chief mechanic signals the driver back into the race with a wave of his arm – and the car is gone almost before you have taken in the fact that all four wheels have been changed. At best, the car has been stationary for only seven or eight seconds!

For the winning mechanics, of course, there is the celebration and feeling of sheer elation at

Left On the grid before the warm-up lap for the 1986 Hungarian Grand Prix. At top right is Senna (Lotus-Renault 98T); at top left is Piquet (Williams-Honda FW11), with team-mate Mansell behind him; Prost (McLaren-TAG MP4/2C) is behind Senna. Back-markers are, at right, Huub Rothengatter (Zakspeed 861) and, at left and last of all, Allen Berg (Osella-Alfa Romeo FA1F).

Above and **right** Two
of the supreme
'quick-change' artists
on the F1 scene go
about their business
during the 1987
season. In the picture
above, Prost's
McLaren pit team; on
the right Senna's
Lotus team. When on
reasonable form, both
teams can expect to
change the tyres and
signal the cars on
their way in between
seven and eight
seconds; the
Williams pit work is
similarly spritely.

being involved with a group of men who have 'got the job done'. But others are less lucky. Accident damage or mechanical failure may have claimed their machines during the course of a race. Perhaps the driver has crashed, in a split second putting at naught all that loving attention lavished on the car over the past ten days or so. It may now lie, bent and buckled, somewhere out on the circuit. Being a race mechanic calls for an enormous amount of resilience in situations like this!

Short-wave radio communication between car and team personnel have made life much easier for the grand-prix mechanic. Until a few years ago, conversation in the pit lane was limited to yells and erratic hand signals: precious little could be heard above the noise of the exhausts. Now the drivers, engineers and mechanics can be seen wearing head sets, calmly discussing practice problems with the minimum of fuss and drama.

With the emphasis on fuel economy in current Formula 1, sometimes apparently minor problems crop up during a race which do not even require the car to stop, but nonetheless demand

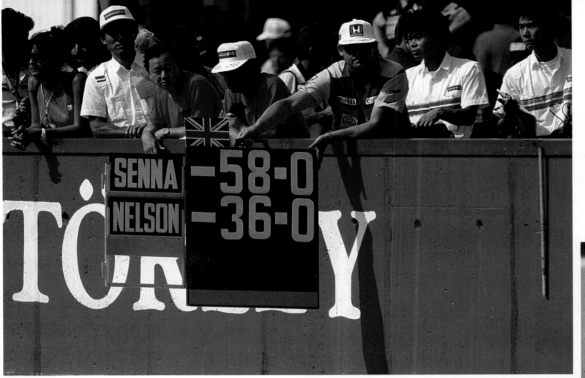

Left The Williams pit team signals to Nigel Mansell during a 1986 race with information about rival Ayrton Senna and team-mate Nelson Piquet.

a close liaison between engineers and drivers.

One of the most remarkable examples of F1 teamwork seen in recent years occurred during the 1987 Belgian Grand Prix at Spa-Franscor-champs and involved the McLaren team. Having an unusually easy time at the head of the field on his way to his 27th grand-prix triumph, Alain Prost was faced with a problem in the cockpit shortly after a typically slick McLaren pit stop for fresh tyres. The digital read-out on the instrument panel of the McLaren suddenly stopped working. All Alain was left with was a rev counter. Deep in the computerised ignition/fuel system, a tiny plug had come out of its socket. There was nothing wrong with the car, but Prost now lacked vital information: he needed to know about his fuel situation – how much he was using and how much he had left. When the plug came adrift, a 'fail-safe' system on the TAG turbo engine automatically adjusted itself to a pre-programmed turbo-boost setting that was different from that at which Prost had been running. Even though he was under no real pressure from his rivals at the time, Prost nonetheless needed the computer's on-going read-out so that he would know the extent to which he would be able to respond to a challenge to his lead without running out of fuel.

Prost spoke to his engineer on his radio link and explained the problem. There was no panic: the pit crew simply got into radio contact with Prost's team-mate Stefan Johansson, who was running second in the other McLaren, and asked him to read out his own (quite satisfactory) fuel-consumption figure. This was relayed to Prost – and he sped on to victory without the slightest further hitch. Nobody would have known about the drama if Prost himself had not mentioned it, almost casually, after the race.

Despite the presence of such electronic gad-getry, the mechanics may well be called upon to

Below *Mansell, like other F1 drivers, can communicate with his pit during a race by means of a radio link. The speaker and earphones are incorporated into his* *helmet. The black stick-like radio aerial can be seen on the nose of the car.*

improvise in certain circumstances. They may have to tape up a driver's broken helmet visor at a panic pit stop, or struggle with a sticking rear-wheel nut, or clear radiator ducts of obstructive paper, or other detritus picked up from the track, which may be threatening to overheat the engine. Whatever the problem, top mechanics are drilled to cope with it methodically and without fuss. To the outsider it looks as though they are taking their time. But the old maxim 'more haste, less speed' applies more pointedly to motor racing than probably to any other high-tech sport.

In little more than an hour and a half the race is over. The winning driver climbs the victor's rostrum, acknowledges the cheers of the crowd by spraying champagne over their heads, and disappears from view. Then the mechanics get on with the business of clearing up the debris. Oil-stained racing cars and a pit garage full of scattered equipment take some gathering together. The hydraulic lift on the back of the articulated transporter is primed ready for use, the cars pumped dry of fuel, and the tyres stripped from their wheel rims for returning to the tyre-company's truck. The cars are given a rub over, checked for any obvious damage and then rolled, one by one, on to the ramp and lifted into the snug interior of the transporter.

Engines are crated up and stowed in their own special compartments between the wheels of the trailer unit, while specialised components are packed in dozens of drawers inside the truck. It is like packing a Chinese puzzle. Within three or four hours the doors are closed, the big diesel's

Below Michele Alboreto's Ferrari F187 makes a quick getaway after a tyre change. The Italian équipe *is rarely as slick at this operation as the British teams.*

Above *Victory for Prost: the McLaren team jubilant as the world champion takes the flag in the 1986 Australian Grand Prix at Adelaide.*

engine booms into life amid a cloud of blue smoke, and the 'big rigs' begin rumbling out of the paddock, headlights picking out the litter and debris scattered across the paddock floor after a day at the races. Ten days later, at some other venue across Europe – or on the other side of the world – the whole complex process of preparing the cars in the pit lane will begin all over again.

This, then, is the mechanics' domain – a workplace staffed by shrewd, adept and committed men, who love machinery and guard their team's reputation and secrets with all the enthusiasm and professionalism displayed by their top-line drivers. The pit lane is a private world with its own conventions, its own gossip, its own procedures. At the end of the day, you can always get another driver. But the respected chief mechanic in the pit lane may well have 20 years' experience under his belt. If he is good, he will be in great demand.

THE RACE

THE PROF PLAYS IT COOL

McLaren Win the Tyre Test

After a five-month lay-off the teams rolled down to Río with the mixture of enthusiasm, hope and foreboding of boys entering a new school term. The new season saw changes. With Pirelli pulling out of Formula 1 at the end of 1986 and Goodyear preoccupied with fighting off a takeover bid, only a late-hour decision by the American tyre company saved the series from disaster. Now everyone was on identical Goodyear rubber (and most teams had to pay for their tyres). Those super-sticky qualifiers were out.

As the first phase of a two-year programme to oust turbos from 1989, normally aspirated 3.5-litre engines were permitted, while the turbos had their power curbed to 4-bar boost, with FISA providing 'pop-off' valves for this purpose. There were rumbles that the valves were inaccurate and could be overridden, but the one team unworried by this were McLaren, who had deliberately opted to run their TAG engines at 3.6 bar. It paid off in the opening round.

There was no chance that the non-turbo brigade could compete with their much more powerful opponents, but to sweeten the pill they were given championships of their own: the Jim Clark Cup for drivers, the Colin Chapman Cup for constructors. Running a two-car team throughout, Ken Tyrrell, with Cosworth DFZ engines, was clear favourite to pick up both pots.

Before practice began there was a burst of ill feeling that had the drivers threatening a boycott. All grand prix drivers have to have a Superlicence, and FISA told them that in addition to the basic charge they would have to pay an extra sum for each point gained during 1986. This meant a hefty bill for drivers who had done well the previous season, and they were understandably miffed at being penalised for doing their job well.

Alain Prost argued for the driver and there were heated words in the torrid Río atmosphere. The outcome was a compromise: the drivers reluctantly agreed to the charges, while FISA promised these would rise only in line with inflation over the next four years.

So it was back to business, and the Honda-engined Williams cars set the pace with Nigel Mansell on pole and teammate Nelson Piquet

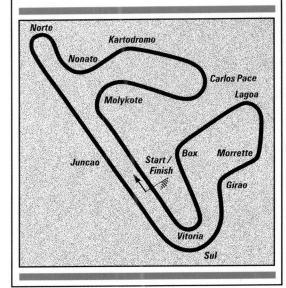

BRAZILIAN GRAND PRIX
— 12 April —

61 laps, 190.7 miles
Down the coast from Río, the Jacarepagua circuit is flat and abrasive. Two long left-hand corners put great strain on the drivers' neck muscles. The heat and humidity is strength-sapping.

alongside. The gulf between the turbos and the atmospherics' was underined by the massive 10-second gap between Mansell's pole lap and the best one by Jonathan Palmer (quickest of the 3.5-litre cars). Ayrton Senna was third on the grid, his Lotus-Honda using a sophisticated computer-controlled 'active-ride' suspension, which Lotus (whose parent firm has pioneered the system) had decided to develop during the season. Only fifth on the grid was twice world champion Prost; but he sounded a warning to his rivals when he was quickest during the race day warm-up.

A problem of the Jacarepagua circuit is its abrasive surface. Most teams expected to pit at least twice for fresh tyres. A driver with a smooth technique has a definite advantage, and Prost,

Left Thierry Boutsen began the season encouragingly, taking his Benetton into fifth place at Río – and placing fourth three weeks later at Imola.

Below Alain Prost earned victory by matchlessly smooth driving, which enabled him to conserve his tyres and pit only twice instead of his rivals' three times on the abrasive Jacarepagua circuit.

Right Nelson Piquet (Williams) took the lead from the start, but had to pit after only seven laps to have rubbish removed from his radiator air intakes; team-mate Nigel Mansell pitted with the same trouble a few laps later.

not known as the 'Professor' for nothing, came out on top in the rubber battle. He managed on two pit stops while rivals needed three.

The Williams duo were pre-race favourites and the excited Brazilian crowd gave Piquet, their local lad, decibels of applause as he swept out into the lead. But not for long. After only seven laps he was into the pits, where tyres were changed while rubbish was hastily removed from air intakes; and it was not long before Mansell pitted with the same problem. The Williams team had clearly blundered by failing to fit mesh guards over the intakes, overlooking the habit of Brazilian spectators to throw waste paper anywhere.

Senna took over the lead from Piquet; but Prost was soon in front, and he regained the lead after his first tyre stop. From then on he was untouchable. He held on to his lead when he came in for his second set of fresh tyres, and drove cannily with fine precision to his 26th Grand Prix win. It was one of Prost's most memorable performances, demonstrating his ice-cool approach and indicating that he firmly intended to hang on to his world title.

Piquet was a distant second, while Mansell, suffering from both an overheating engine and a puncture which cost valuable time, eventually picked up on championship point with sixth place.

Senna seemed to have something of a struggle with his 'active' Lotus, but a dogged effort which promised to bring points came to naught when his engine failed. His new Japanese teammate, Satoru Nakajima, finished just out of the points.

Stefan Johansson, late of Ferrari, backed up the McLaren effort with third place, finishing ahead of Gerhard Berger, who had replaced him in the Italian team. The elegant Benettons, now with the Ford turbo engine, promised well, but Teo Fabi was an early retirement. Thierry Boutsen, however, was a worthy fifth after a frightening moment when a tyre burst at the end of the main straight.

First home in the non-turbo battle was Jonathan Palmer, on this occasion having a one-off drive but soon to be confirmed as a regular Tyrrell driver.

The McLaren team had lost John Barnard, lured to Ferrari, but their depth of technical strength gave them the promise of continuing success. And, now he was within hailing distance of Jackie Stewart's 27 GP wins, Prost was determined to get into the record books.

1 Alain Prost (McLaren-TAG MP4/3)	1h 39m 45.141s, 114.699mph
2 Nelson Piquet (Williams-Honda FW11B)	1h 40m 25.688s
3 Stefan Johansson (McLaren-TAG MP4/3)	1h 40m 41.899s
4 Gerhard Berger (Ferrari F1/87)	1h 41m 24.376s
5 Thierry Boutsen (Benetton-Ford B187)	1 lap down
6 Nigel Mansell (Williams-Honda FW11B)	1 lap down

Fastest lap *Piquet, 1m 33.861s, 119.901mph*

MANSELL BY A MILE

Piquet Sits It Out

It would need a miracle to carve out a Grand Prix circuit in the tiny self-governing principality of San Marino. But they have held a Grand Prix each year since 1981, staged some 45 miles away at Imola. They get the publicity rub-off for their tourist industry, while the Italians get two grands prix (which makes one wonder why Britain, with such a strong motor-race following, cannot have two as well).

The circuit at Imola, named after Dino Ferrari, Enzo Ferrari's son who died tragically young, is a crafty concoction that offers a considerable challenge not only to drivers but also to engineers trying to find the right balance between competitive power and fuel thirst. Solving this tricky equation depends crucially on the man in the cockpit, and in this department Prost is superb. He had won this grand prix three years running (though excluded from the 1985 results when his car was found to be a trifle underweight), and after the heady success of Brazil he was tipped to win again.

In good form during qualifying and third on the grid, the little Frenchman was delighted with his McLaren, which had been virtually untested before Brazil but had undergone fine tuning in the days before San Marino.

Although Nigel Mansell swooped into the lead, past Senna, on the second lap, Prost made his habitual steady progress, lying second after five laps and beginning to close on Mansell. Then the famed reliability of his McLaren let him down: the alternator belt-drive failed and he was out of the race.

With the disappearance of that menace from his rear-view mirror, Mansell sailed to his first victory of the season, losing his lead for only a few laps after pitting for tyres but then drawing away to win from Senna by nearly half a minute. For Mansell it was not as easy as it appeared from the trackside. He had planned to drive hard at the start in order to build up a substantial lead

SAN MARINO GRAND PRIX
— 3 May —

59 laps, 184.8 miles
The Dino Ferrari circuit is named after Enzo Ferrari's late son and is on the outskirts of Imola. Very hard on brakes and notoriously tough on fuel consumption.

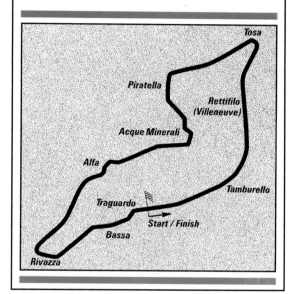

Left Nigel Mansell (Williams) dominated the race, despite losing pole position to Ayrton Senna when Honda technicians tinkered with his engine computer during practice.

Below Italian fans went wild when Michele Alboreto (Ferrari) led for three laps after Mansell pitted for fresh tyres. Alboreto finished third, but Ferrari had not won in 25 races.

before easing back the turbo boost to ensure he did not run out of fuel. This he did, but a lost wheel balance weight caused a vibration which brought him in for his tyre change earlier than he had wished. Later, he had a near miss overtaking a back marker and went on to grass when his brakes played tricks at one of the chicanes.

Just with the Prost threat out of the way, he had little difficulty dealing with the rest of the opposition. And the man who could have offered his main opposition – team-mate Piquet – was sitting in a TV commentary box, his crash during practice two days earlier having left him concussed. (It had been a horrendous high-speed shunt; and that Piquet was able to walk away,

albeit groggily, was tribute to the toughness of his Williams.) After spending the night under observaton in hospital, Piquet insisted he was fit to drive, but following considerable debate he had to bow to medical advice.

Piquet's accident brought another repercussion. The Goodyear boffins had earlier spotted tyre blistering on some cars, and since it was thought just a possibility that Piquet's accident had resulted from a tyre failure, they scrapped all their stock at Imola and flew in several hundred replacement tyres from Wolverhampton overnight.

Team Lotus seemed to have made progress with their innovative suspension, but Senna was unable to match Mansell's race pace (even though he put in his usual masterful qualifying lap to take pole). Lotus and Williams were, of course, using similar Honda engines, and it seemed that the Lotus was less competitive because of its greater weight and lower aerodynamic efficiency.

The frenetic fans at Imola, for whom nothing but a Ferrari matters, had their prancing horse flags waving vigorously as Michele Alboreto diced with Senna (and led for three laps). There was the prospect of second place for the red car, but lost boost pressure (an all-too-common Ferrari failing the previous season) slowed Alboreto and he had to be content with third.

1	Nigel Mansell (Williams-Honda FW11B)	1h 31m 24.076s, 121.292mph
2	Ayrton Senna (Lotus-Honda 99T)	1h 31m 51.621s
3	Michele Alboreto (Ferrari F1/87)	1h 32m 03.220s
4	Stefan Johansson (McLaren-TAG MP4/3)	1h 32m 24.664s
5	Martin Brundle (Zakspeed 871)	2 laps down
6	Satoru Nakajima (Lotus-Honda 99T)	2 laps down

Fastest lap *Teo Fabi (Benetton-Ford B187), 1m 29.246s, 126.326mph*

Left Nelson Piquet's San Marino ended at Friday's practice, when he crashed at 180mph at Tamburello corner. Concussed but with no broken bones, he spent the race as guest commentator for Italian television.

Below Martin Brundle gave the Zakspeed 871 its debut at Imola. Though suffering from brake problems, he managed fifth place to gain the first GP points for the German équipe.

Stefan Johansson also lost a possible second place, having to make an extra stop to replace a broken front wing and plate. He was fourth, while two laps down were Martin Brundle for Zakspeed and Satoru Nakajima in the second Lotus. Brundle brought Zakspeed their first points by taking fifth, and Nakajima became the first Japanese driver to score a championship point.

There was big disappointment for Derek Warwick. Only four laps from the end, his Arrows was lying fifth when the Imola jinx struck again and he ran out of fuel.

Riccardo Patrese surprised everyone by running second for several laps around mid-distance and then again some laps later. It looked like a turnround for the low-line Brabham, but the car faded to finish ninth. Officially, the reason was a fuel sensor problem; but it seemed more likely that Patrese held his prominent position only by using high boost, leading inevitably to a fuel crisis that forced him to slow down.

This time it was Philippe Streiff's turn to head the normally aspirated groups in his Tyrrell, while Palmer retired with clutch trouble.

But the day belonged to Mansell. Granted he had profited from Piquet's absence and Prost's retirement, but he had given a commanding display and now headed the drivers' championship.

GIFT-WRAPPED FOR PROST

Aggro On and Off the Track

Motor racing is packed with might-have-beens. In 1987 the splendid Spa-Francorchamps circuit, winding trough the beautiful Ardennes, produced a vintage example of the geure.

It all happened on lap two. It did not involve the front-runners, but it led directly to a later incident that saw Mansell and Senna tangle on the track (and tangle again in a sorry incident in the pits). And the upshot was that Prost was handed his 27th Grand Prix victory on a plate.

Senna had beaten Mansell in the 1985 GP and Mansell returned the compliment the next year. Could either win again this time? Mansell was in scorching form during qualifying, setting pole no less than 2.3 seconds quicker than Piquet had managed the year before with qualifying tyres and unlimited turbo boost.

When the race began Mansell made a super start and led by some two seconds at the end of lap one. It looked like another Mansell-dominating drive. ... But on lap two Philippe Streiff's Tyrrell snapped out of control, slammed at high speed into a barrier and littered the track with debris. Team-mate Jonathan Palmer could not avoid the wreckage and his car was also badly damaged. In other incidents four more cars were damaged, with Thierry Boutsen's Benetton hitting Gerhard Berger's spinning Ferrari and René Arnoux's Ligier tangling with Andréa De Cesaris's Brabham.

The race was halted and re-run over the full distance, with all but Palmer driving spare cars. From the re-start Senna surged into the lead, but half-way round the first lap, as Mansell tried to overtake, the two cars touched and both went off. Senna was bogged down in the gravel trap, and though Mansell got away, he retired later with underbody damage.

Opinions differ as to who was at fault. Each blamed the other. But what happened later was uncalled for: Mansell strode to the Lotus pits and Senna found himself being physically assaulted by the Englishman, who had to be restrained by mechanics.

It was a tasteless episode and the media made much of it. Criticism was heaped upon Mansell, and his reputation was marred, as was that of motor sport. It simply should not have happened.

The result of the accident was that Piquet found himself the leader with Alboreto lying second. The Ferrari pair had shown improved performance during qualifying, with Berger and Alboreto fourth and fifth on the grid. But the Italian cars were still showing fragility: Berger's engine broke early on, and Alboreto was sidelined a little later with transmission failure.

Piquet must have been thanking his stars with his two rivals out of contention, but it was not to be a Williams day; he, too, retired after a few laps through a complicated problem which began with bolts working adrift on a turbo unit.

BELGIAN GRAND PRIX
— 17 May —

43 laps, 185.4 miles

The Spa-Francorchamps circuit is on public roads in the Ardennes. A true driver's course, packed with challenge and calling for real engine power. Dogged by unpredictable weather.

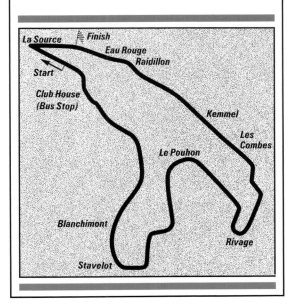

Above Philippe Streiff (Tyrrell) crashed at Eau Rouge on lap 2. Team-mate Jonathan Palmer, close behind, could not avoid him. Palmer's car is seen being taken from the track.

Opposite Nigel Mansell made a great start at Spa. He's seen here at Eau Rouge on the first lap, pursued by Senna, Piquet, the Ferraris of Alboreto and Gerhard Berger, and Prost.

Above *Alain Prost (here on a practice lap) kept his head in spite of a broken computer and took his 27th GP victory after rivals Mansell and Senna tried to occupy the same piece of road and Piquet's turbo-sensor packed up.*

After that it was the cool-thinking Prost all the way to the flag. But even he was not granted a smooth run. The fuel read-out in his McLaren went on the blink and he became concerned about his consumption rate.

He radioed his pit and asked for information about the consumption being recorded by his team-mate, Stefan Johansson. Communication was difficult and he picked up messages from the pit only occasionally. But, with Johansson lapping behind him in second place at around the same speed he correctly assumed that he was driving within his fuel limit.

The earlier incidents, on track and in the Lotus pit, tended to overshadow Prost's victory, but at least he had achieved a major ambition of equalling Jackie Stewart's 27 GP firsts (and drew from Stewart the comment that he was the complete Grand Prix driver – easily the best of the current bunch).

The Ferraris were not the only team to show promise before failing. Much had been expected of the Benettons, especially with Thierry Boutsen racing before his home crowd. Both Boutsen and Teo Fabi made good use of the fine handling qualities of the Rory Byrne-designed chassis, but after strong runs both retired with mechanical problems.

The erratic Andrea de Cesaris had one of his rare error-free races, and drove his Brabham into third place, although finishing a lap down with his petrol tank dry when he crossed the line.

American-born Eddie Cheever (Arrows) came home fourth, just managing to keep the advantage over Nakajima, whose Lotus ran into gearbox trouble in the closing laps. René Arnoux, so often involved in controversial incidents, scraped into sixth place in a Ligier which had been hastily adapted to take a Megatron (née BMW) unit before the previous GP after Alfa Romeo refused to supply their engines following critical remarks from the fiery Frenchman. We did not know then, but it was to be the only point he or the Ligier team would gain all season.

This time Philippe Alliot won the 'second division' 3.5-litre battle in a Lola, but he was three laps behind the winner, underlining the performance differential between the turbos and the rest.

1 Alain Prost (McLaren-TAG MP4/3)		1h 27m 03.217s, 127.803mph
2 Stefan Johansson (McLaren-TAG MP4/3)		1h 27m 27.981s
3 Andrea de Cesaris (Brabham-BMW BT56)		1 lap down
4 Eddie Cheever (Arrows-Megatron A10)		1 lap down
5 Satoru Nakajima (Lotus-Honda 99T)		1 lap down
6 René Arnoux (Ligier-Megatron JS29B)		2 laps down
Fastest lap Prost, 1m 57.153s, 132.513mph (record)		

So ended a day packed with the kind of drama and incident the sport can do without. But it was also one that put Alain Prost on a pedestal beside Jackie Stewart. And no one was betting against him breaking the Scotsman's record before the season was over.

Below *Wet-weather buff Eddie Cheever (Arrows) made the most of a downpour in practice to set up his car. Eleventh on the grid, he finished an excellent fourth.*

SENNA
SEES IT THROUGH

First Win for New Suspension

Below Ayrton Senna negotiates Loew's hairpin. From here the circuit winds downhill to the right-hander at Portier, the tunnel and the harbour.

Above Soon after the start, Ivan Capelli (March, left) forces Satoru Nakajima (Lotus, centre) and Philippe Alliot (Lola) wide. They are followed by Martin Brundle (Zakspeed) and Piercarlo Ghinzani (Ligier).

Monaco is without doubt the glamour circuit, the venue that attracts the rich flaunting their wealth with yachts and luxury cars as well as the sport's real enthusiasts who can feel part of the action within the confines of the tiny principality.

It is twisty and narrow and has its short-comings, both for drivers, for whom there are few opportunities for overtaking, and for the teams, who have to toil in a makeshift paddock by the side of the harbour. But for its magnetic public appeal and its value to sponsors it would surely have been banished from the grand prix calendar years ago.

For many years only 16 cars were allowed on the grid. Later this was raised to 20. For 1987 it was decreed by FISA that the limit should be 26, as with all the other championship races. This brought protests from the top teams, who com-plained that the extra traffic could be dangerous and that, with the problems of overtaking the slower cars – and particularly the non-turbo machines – there was bound to be baulking and bashing.

The complaints went unheeded. FOCA supremo Bernie Ecclestone declared tersely, 'Accidents are not caused by cars on the track but by what drivers do in the cockpit, and unfortunately idiots will always be idiots.'

Best pleased were those outsiders who, in a more restricted field, would have failed to qualify. Most of them were now certain to get into the race and so delight their sponsors in this most heavily media-swamped event.

The critics, however, felt they had made their point during practice when Michele Alboreto tried to force his Ferrari past Christian Danner's Zakspeed going up the hill to Casino Square. Though neither driver was hurt, the Ferrari was

---

MONACO GRAND PRIX
— 31 May —

78 laps, 161.3 miles
The glamour circuit, run over public roads through the principality. Few overtaking opportunities and no respite for drivers: a good grid position is vital.

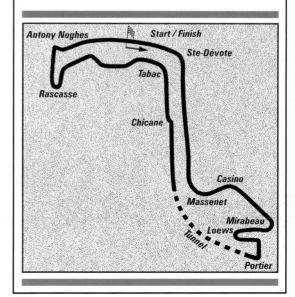

a complete write-off. Looked at objectively, this shunt could not be blamed on heavy traffic – but it resulted in a little bit of motor-racing history. The authorities went into a huddle and disqualified Danner from the meeting, the first time such an action had been taken since the world-championship series began. It was a harsh decision and cynics suggested it would not have happened if Alboreto had been involved with another top driver. The starters were further reduced when the Spanish driver Adrian Campos (Minardi) had an accident and he was not allowed to race on medical grounds.

So the field was down to 24. And with Nigel Mansell and Ayrton Senna – who had reluctantly followed orders to shake hands in the pits – ranged on the front row of the grid many wondered whether they would have another barging match.

Mansell, that Belgian incident forgotten, had been terrific in practice and qualified yards faster than anyone. When the lights turned to green there was no question of a first-corner fracas between the two great rivals. Mansell simply roared his Williams into an impressive lead. After 10 laps he was nearly 12 seconds ahead of Senna and clearly king of the streets.

Piquet, in the other Williams, lagged behind in third place. He does not hide his dislike for the circuit (even though he lives in Monaco), and he was still feeling the effects of his San Marino crash.

The Mansell fairytale evaporated abruptly after 29 laps, when he slowed to a halt: a broken weld had brought about a lack of turbo boost. It was a sad conclusion to a brilliant display, and Senna swept on to the first victory by a car with active-ride suspension. Piquet, still in subdued form, profited from Mansell's retirement to take second place, more than half a minute behind.

The Ferrari fans, who swarm over the nearby Italian frontier in their thousands, had plenty to shout about. Alboreto shrugged off his practice crash to snatch third place, with team-mate Gerhard Berger fourth. Alain Prost, winner in the three previous years, was out of luck this time. His TAG engine was sick almost from the start and finally expired three laps from the finish when he was lying third. Stefan Johansson, too, retired his McLaren with engine trouble.

Ken Tyrrell had forecast that at least one of his drivers would be in the points. The 3.5-litre Cosworth DFZ engine was less powerful than the turbos but the Tyrrells were lighter and more nimble round the many corners and the egines more responsive. Jonathan Palmer proved the point, driving impeccably and with tremendous dash. With 19 laps to go, as the turbos took turns to expire, he lay sixth, and with Prost's late retirement moved up to fifth. It was the first time he had gained championship points after 43 grands prix; and Ivan Capelli added to the delight in the camps of the 'atmospherics' by bringing his March home sixth.

Although pre-race pundits had prophesied carnage if the two types of cars were allowed to mix on this circuit, the only race accident was to Philippe Streiff's Tyrrell – and that was due to a brake failure. Team Lotus had proved that their suspension worked well on a slow circuit, giving their drivers an easier ride and therefore less fatigue. Senna looked forward to the next round in Detroit with some confidence.

Below *After his close call Capelli must have been relieved to get to the top of the hill at Massenet. He went on to finish in sixth place – his best result of the season.*

1	Ayrton Senna (Lotus-Honda 99T)	1h 57m 54.085s, 82.084mph
2	Nelson Piquet (Williams-Honda FW11B)	1h 58m 27.297s
3	Michele Alboreto (Ferrari F1/87)	1h 59m 06.924s
4	Gerhard Berger (Ferrari F1/87)	1 lap down
5	Jonathan Palmer (Tyrrell-Cosworth DG/016)	2 laps down
6	Ivan Capelli (March-Cosworth 871)	2 laps down

Fastest lap Senna, 1m 27.685s, 84.901mph

Above Senna's victory marked the first win for the Lotus active-suspension system. He made the fastest lap of the race and had more than half a minute to spare over Nelson Piquet's Williams.

AYRTON
KING OF THE STREETS

'Active' Smoothes Motown Bumps

Below *Nelson Piquet (Williams) stormed back from 18th place, following a puncture on lap 1, to take second place – a remarkable effort on a circuit he detests.*

The Detroit circuit is, to say the least, unloved by both drivers and the teams. For the 1987 Grand Prix some of the more notorious bumps had been ironed out; but most of the track is claustrophobic, there are no permanent pit facilities, and there is usually oppressive heat and humidity in June. Alain Prost was on record saying he would much prefer the race to go back to Watkins Glen; he felt the slow Detroit track setting did nothing to encourage the American public to savour true grand prix racing. The only driver who seemed to revel in it was Mansell, who, as at Monaco, displayed his talents as a street fighter. Once more he was stunningly fast in qualifying, grabbing pole three quarters of a second faster than Senna. It was his fourth pole in five races.

The prospect of another early-race duel was on the cards but (again as in Monaco) Mansell roared off to pull away from the bunch, gaining a second a lap over Senna.

Surely he could not be jinxed again? Oh yes, he could! At one point Mansell led by over 20 seconds, and as he eased back to save fuel and conserve his car Senna gradually began to chip away at his advantage. It was over half race distance before Mansell came in for tyres. And that was when his troubles began. A rear wheel nut jammed, costing him some 10 seconds more than usual. Senna took over the lead and Mansell was now third, behind Prost. Soon, though, he had taken Prost and was really flying. He was more than 20 seconds behind Senna, but on fresh tyres. Assuming Senna still had to stop for tyres, Mansell looked comfortably placed.

But it soon became apparent that something was wrong. The precise Mansell control was lacking and his lap times became erratic. Was there something amiss with his Williams? No – this time it was Mansell himself in trouble, with

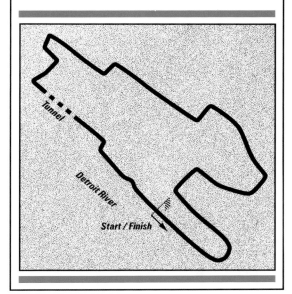

DETROIT GRAND PRIX
— 21 June —

63 laps, 157.5 miles

A tortuous track running through Motown's public streets and surrounded by forbidding concrete walls. Lots of slow corners putting stress on transmissions, and tough on brakes.

Below *Gerhard Berger damaged his Ferrari in practice and started in twelfth place on the grid. But by the seventh lap he was in sixth place and he finished in fourth – the last unlapped runner in the race.*

severe leg cramp. Several times Mansell thought he would have to give up, but he soldiered on in pain, unable to keep up a competitive pace and eventually finishing fifth. When he rolled to a halt he had to be lifted from the cockpit, thoroughly exhausted and bitterly disappointed.

Even had he been fit there is doubt whether he would have caught Senna, for the Brazilian went through on one set of tyres. Senna's Lotus suspension was giving him a better ride over the bumps and he was less tired than his rivals. After Mansell made his pit stop Senna learned over the radio that the Williams' tyres were not too badly worn and would probably have lasted the race. So he throttled back to make his tyres last and cantered home well ahead of Piquet in the other Williams.

Soon after the start of the race Piquet had looked right out of contention: he had a puncture, which dumped him back in 18th place. Then he began a determined drive which demonstrated that, despite his dislike of the circuit and suggestions that he lacked some of his old sparkle, he had lost none of his motivation. Though still feeling the effects of his Imola accident, which were still giving him sleepless nights, he gave a memorable performance.

The Benetton team were anxious for a good showing in front of the Ford hierarchy. But although their revised Ford engines, giving improved throttle response, enabled Thierry Boutsen to claim fourth spot on the grid, neither he nor Teo Fabi figured in the results. Boutsen, a useful fourth for a time, fell victim to brake trouble; Fabi, involved in a tigerish battle with Eddie Cheever's Arrows, ripped off his nose cone and had to retire when it could not be replaced. Cheever recovered and charged through the field to finish sixth.

Both McLaren drivers had complained of lack of grip and Prost was grateful when Alboreto's Ferrari slowed to retire with transmission trouble. Prost, too, had a gearbox problem but managed to finish third, ahead of Berger's Ferrari.

There was plenty of Motown mayhem that afternoon. Philippe Streiff lost a wheel after his Tyrrell hit a wall; so too did Derek Warwick in his Arrows and Philippe Alliot in the Lola. But the most spectacular performance came from Nakajima – and he shared it with the whole world. His Lotus carried a TV camera and viewers had the best possible view of exactly how you should not start a race on a narrow circuit. An over-enthusiastic Nakajima, starting from near the back of the grid, was far too lead-footed in the heavy traffic. At the second corner he rode over the rear of Ivan Capelli's March and within seconds was embroiled with Campos in a Minardi. It made wonderful television – but Lotus team chief Peter Warr managed to restrain a smile.

Senna had now overtaken Prost to take the championship lead, while Piquet, with three second places from four outings, was a steady third in the list. Mansell was trailing at this stage but looking forward with relish to the faster track at Paul Ricard, where he had won the year before and was confident he could win again.

Below Alessandro Nannini (Minardi) enters the tunnel at Detroit. His engine expired after 22 laps, when he had reached tenth place.

1 Ayrton Senna (Lotus-Honda 99T)	1h 50m 16.358s, 85.697mph
2 Nelson Piquet (Williams-Honda FW11B)	1h 50m 50.177s
3 Alain Prost (McLaren-TAG MP4/3)	1h 51m 01.685s
4 Gerhard Berger (Ferrari F1/87)	1h 51m 18.959s
5 Nigel Mansell (Williams-Honda FW11B)	1 lap down
6 Eddie Cheever (Arrows-Megatron A10)	3 laps down

Fastest lap *Senna, 1m 40.464s, 89.584mph (record)*

Above *Senna, seen here in front of Motown's grandiose Renaissance Center, found the Lotus active suspension ironed out the notoriously bumpy city circuit and he cruised home for his second Detroit win in succession.*

MANSELL MAKES HIS COMEBACK

Battles of the Team-Mates

The Paul Ricard circuit, laid out on a rocky plateau in the hills above the French riviera resort of Bandol, has little to offer the spectator. It is flat and bare, lacks atmosphere, and the crowds are kept at a very respectful distance from the action on safety grounds. For the drivers, though, it was a considerable relief to be back on a 'real' race circuit, with a 200mph-plus straight and fast, demanding curves after the Mickey Mouse circuits at Monaco and Detroit.

Mansell soon demonstrated that he was equally at home on a fast track, setting the pace throughout practice, taking pole position, and proving as dominant in qualifying as Senna had been in 1986. This was hardly surprising since the Honda turbo had a power advantage over its rivals. But Prost raised eyebrows when

FRENCH GRAND PRIX

— 5 July —

80 laps, 189.5 miles

Set on a rocky plateau a few miles from the Mediterranean, the Paul Ricard circuit is clinical and fast but lacking in atmosphere; shortened to 2.37 miles in 1986.

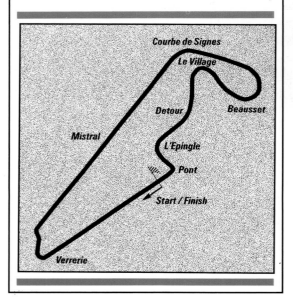

Below Nigel Mansell was completely in charge at Paul Ricard, taking pole and winning comfortably. Here he leads Prost, Senna and Piquet, who took second place and broke the lap record.

Right Philippe Streiff (Tyrrell) was last but one on the grid but finished in sixth place — one ahead of team-mate Jonathan Palmer.

he qualified second fastest. The double world champion's McLaren had less power from its TAG engine but the chassis was working like a dream. Given a healthy machine Prost looked to post a threat. But the race, run under a hot Provence sun, saw Prost soon struggling with a racalcitrant engine; he made a game fight of it but eventually landed a distant third place.

Although using the same Honda engine as the Williams, Senna's Lotus was clearly no match for the Patrick Head-designed car. Team Lotus felt they have made improvements in the mapping of their 'trick' suspension to meet the demands of the faster circuits, but inferior aerodynamics and greater weight worked against them.

For Senna the euphoria of the previous two GPs was over; he finished fourth, a lap behind, and knew already that he would have a tough job grabbing the championship. This was to be a Williams day, Mansell versus Piquet with no holds barred. There was growing rivalry between the two team-mates and more than mere rumblings of personal animosity. Mansell held Piquet at bay for quite a time, with Prost keeping both of them on their tes. When Piquet made an error Prost swooped into second place and that was the order when the trio began their tyre stops. Piquet was first into the pits after 30 laps, and six laps later the other two changed tyres. The order then became Piquet, Prost, Mansell; but Mansell soon overtook Prost to lie second.

There followed a gripping duel for the lead between the two yellow-and-blue cars. If there were any team orders regarding priority the drivers ignored them.

Mansell was pressing hard, waiting for Piquet to make a mistake. It came on lap 46, when Piquet ran slightly wide at the Beausset right-hander, and the Englishman seized his chance. He dived inside the Brazilian and took the lead which he held to the finish. Piquet later complained that unless he had given Mansell room there would have been an accident, but it was generally agreed he had made an error under pressure.

In the 1986 race the Williams team had stolen a march on their rivals by making two pit stops, calculating that time lost in the pits would be made up by a faster pace on fresh tyres. Desperate to claw back the lead, Piquet decided to repeat the manoeuvre this time. On fresh tyres perhaps he could make up the deficit. So, with 17 laps to go, he played what he hoped would be his trump card ... but the gamble failed. His stop cost nearly 16 seconds at standstill – double the normal time – after his engine stalled, and though he soon retrieved second place from Prost and set a new lap record he just could not close the gap. Piquet did slash a big chunk out of

Mansell's lead but Mansell, despite having to change gear with the gear lever stub when the knob came adrift, was able to pace himself to his second win of the season while Piquet had to be satisfied with yet another second place – his fourth so far.

The other possible challengers, Benetton and Ferrari, flattered only to disappoint. For Ferrari, Alboreto, with a dragging clutch, jumped the start and was penalised 60 seconds (it made no difference because later his engine broke); Berger muffed his start from sixth on the grid, dragged himself as high as fifth, but spun off with a few laps to go when part of his suspension failed.

The Benettons were expected to excel on this faster track, but Boutsen, fifth on the grid, retired before half distance when lying fifth. Team-mate Fabi managed to salvage fifth place but only just made it home, three laps down, with a broken driveshaft.

Above Great determination paid off for Teo Fabi (Benetton). After enduring several mechanical failures during practice, he brought his car in to take fifth place despite breaking a driveshaft.

Two other team-mates, Palmer and Streiff, also had their private battle, with Streiff gaining his first world-championship point and Palmer seventh. With less than half the season's races run the Tyrrell team was well ahead of any rival for the Colin Chapman Cup for 'unblown' constructors, while the drivers' award – the Jim Clark Cup – looked certain to be decided between the two Tyrrell pilots, with Palmer perhaps having an edge.

With six rounds gone Senna was in the lead with 27 points, one ahead of Prost; Piquet was on 24 and Mansell 21. At this stage it seemed the drivers' championship must go to one of this quartet, and with the British Grand Prix a week hence Mansell's many fans were sure he could narrow the gap. The Williams cars showed in France they had the legs of the opposition, so everyone was asking which of the two would win at Silverstone.

1 Nigel Mansell (Williams-Honda FW11B)		1h 37m 03.839s, 117.165mph
2 Nelson Piquet (Williams-Honda FW11B)		1h 37m 11.550s
3 Alain Prost (McLaren-TAG MP4/3)		1h 37m 59.094s
4 Ayrton Senna (Lotus-Honda 99T)		1 lap down
5 Teo Fabi (Benetton-Ford B187)		3 laps down
6 Philippe Streiff (Tyrrell-Cosworth DG/016)		3 laps down

Fastest lap *Piquet, 1m 09.548s, 122.641mph (record)*

ANOTHER 1-2 FOR WILLIAMS

Nigel's Treat for the Fans

They thronged to Silverstone in their tens of thousands, packing every possible vantage point and hoping 'Our Nige' would show all his rivals the way home. Mansell had won the two previous GPs on British soil – the 1985 European GP and the 1986 British GP, both at Brands Hatch – and his fans were hungry for a hat-trick. The Williams-Hondas were clearly the pace-makers but could Mansell hold off Piquet's challenge?

Upset by suggestions that he had lost his motivaton, Piquet had earlier staged a press conference where he insisted he was enjoying his motor racing and certainly did not consider retiring at the end of the season. He underlined that, and disappointed Mansell fans, by snatching pole from his team-mate after Mansell's final qualifying effort ended in a ferocious spin. Behind them on the grid it was the now familiar pattern. Senna was next up for Lotus, followed by Prost's McLaren and the Benetton-Fords of Boutsen and Fabi, who were ahead of the two Ferraris.

Prost got away first at the start but not for long. The Williams pair stormed past him on the opening lap and after that it was Williams v Williams all the way. Piquet was in determined mood. After 10 laps he led Mansell by three seconds. Mansell cut into that margin but then began to fall back; his car sounded healthy but something was clearly wrong. Mansell told his team by radio that he was suffering a vibration problem. He soldiered on but the vibration worsened and became so bad he could hardly focus on the next corner.

Before the race the Goodyear technicians had analysed tyre wear and suggested wheel changes should not be necessary. So Mansell was loath to stop since it would put him further behind Piquet. But the vibration was too bad to consider continuing. On lap 35 he came in for fresh rubber. The stop cost him 9.5 seconds, but getting into and out of the pits meant he was now nearly half a minute behind Piquet.

It looked a hopeless task but Mansell drove to the absolute limit in a thrilling display that had the crowd in raptures. Ten laps after his stop, with 20 to go, he was still more than 21 seconds behind. Surely he would have to settle for second place this time?

Below *Sparks fly as Nigel Mansell, his Williams (right) weighed down by a full tank, races neck and neck with team-mate Nelson Piquet in the early laps. At the end, winner Mansell had a two-second lead over Piquet.*

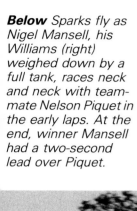

Above *Derek Warwick (Arrows) held off Teo Fabi's Benetton (right) to take fifth place. Both suffered problems —* *Warwick with vibrations and Fabi with an over-thirsty engine.*

BRITISH GRAND PRIX
12 July

65 laps, 192.9 miles
Silverstone circuit, on the site of a wartime airfield, is flat and very fast. The track was modified for the 1987 GP, with a sharp left–right replacing the Woodcote chicane.

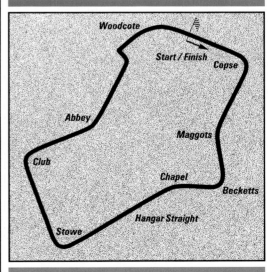

With 22 laps to go Piquet's pit had given him the 'Tyres OK' signal but the scorching pace was telling on his tyres which began to deteriorate. This was revealed in the rapidly closing gap as Mansell pulled out all the stops. Starting lap 63, Mansell was less than a second behind and the din from the excited crowd almost drowned the noise of the engines. Although his fuel read-out looked ominous, Mansell knew he had to go for broke.

Down Hangar Straight he was up to Piquet's exhausts. Aware of the threat, Piquet kept to his line on the right, until Mansell sold him a dummy and feinted as though to overtake on the outside at the right-hand Stowe Corner. Piquet fell for the manoeuvre, edged over to the left to block the threat and left just enough room for Mansell to scrape through on the inside as they so nearly locked wheels. With his tyres going off

Below Andrea de Cesaris escaped unhurt when his Brabham succumbed to a spectacular engine-bay fire caused by a fuel-line fracture on lap 9.

rapidly, Piquet could not make any reply and Mansell went on to his third win of the season, by two seconds.

But it had been a close-run thing. Mansell's long ten-tenths effort had swigged the fuel. On his final lap his engine had coughed, indicating he was short of petrol, and he ran completely dry on his cooling-down lap.

The pleasure of the crowd knew no bounds. They swarmed on to the track in scenes more reminiscent of Monza, and on his lap of honour Mansell stopped to kiss the track at Stowe .He had had his share of ill luck in earlier races. This time fortune had smiled. His clutch had failed in the pre-race warm-up and that vibration, the result of a lost balance-weight, had against the odds given him just the edge on fresher tyres during the final chase.

The 'home' victory overshadowed all else that

day at Silverstone. Senna's less-competitive Lotus brought him third and Satoru Nakajima made it a Honda 1–2–3–4 in the other Lotus. Prost's effort came to a halt 12 laps from the end, when he was lying fourth; but Derek Warwick gave British fans another treat by bringing his Arrows in fifth – his first world championship points for two seasons.

Both Ferraris failed to finish; Berger spun into retirement early on and Alboreto's hopes of a few points disappeared when his rear suspension failed. The Benettons had opted for reliability rather than pace and, with both drivers foxed by duff information which suggested overheating engines, Fabi picked up an undistinguished sixth, with Boutsen seventh. Palmer won the 'second division' battle and took a useful lead in the Jim Clark Cup struggle.

But the day belonged to Mansell, who had done

all his admirers could ask for, and now lay equal second with Piquet in the championship, only one point behind Senna. His prospects for the next round on the fast Hockenheim circuit looked good.

Above Nigel Mansell takes a well-earned swig of water after his second win in two weeks.

1 Nigel Mansell (Williams-Honda FW11B)	1h 19m 11.780s, 146.208mph	
2 Nelson Piquet (Williams-Honda FW11B)	1h 19m 13.698s	
3 Ayrton Senna (Lotus-Honda 99T)	2 laps down	
4 Satoru Nakajima (Lotus-Honda 99T)	2 laps down	
5 Derek Warwick (Arrows-Megatron A10)	2 laps down	
6 Teo Fabi (Benetton-Ford B187)	2 laps down	

Fastest lap *Mansell, 1m 09.832s, 153.059mph (record for revised circuit)*

PIQUET FIRST — AT LAST!

Field Day for the 'Atmospherics'

Above Stefan Johansson (McLaren) took second place when he finished on three tyres and dodgy suspension.

Until this eighth round — the half-way point in the championship — Piquet had been an indefatigable bridesmaid, but never the bride: in six starts (he'd missed San Marino) he had landed five second places.

Playing the percentages was all very well (Keke Rosberg won the 1982 title with only a single victory); but though Piquet was totting up valuable points, he desperately wanted to win to show he could be the master.

On the flat, clinical Hockenheim track which is so hard on engines, Piquet finally saw the chequered flag — but he had to admit he was lucky. Until near the end of the race he had been outstripped convincingly by Prost, whose McLaren had been given a revised and much improved TAG engine. There seemed no way Piquet could get on to terms with Prost and prevent him from logging his 28th Grand Prix win to top Jackie Stewart's record.

In the crowded press tribune the GP reporters were mentally rehearsing their opening lines

('Prost finally achieves his ambition ...' and so on). Suddenly there were groans from the crowd packed into the vast concrete amphitheatre area when Prost failed to appear with less than five laps to go. He had pulled off on to the grass at the far end of the circuit, his alternator drive-belt broken.

Hardly able to believe his good fortune, Piquet cruised to a comfortable victory which sent him to the top of the championship table. Fortunate, yes; but Piquet had showed dogged spirits during what had been a troubled race. On a track where engines are almost continuously at full bore, fuel consumption is a vital factor. (Both McLarens had run dry on their final lap the previous year.) Early on, Piquet's on-board read-out went blank. So far as fuel consumption was concerned he was virtually driving blind; he was receiving some information by radio from his pit, but felt he had to drive cautiously to make certain. After 26 more laps his VDU resumed working, but by that time he was well behind and but for Prost's late failure he would have had to settle for second place yet again.

Following the euphoria of Silverstone, Mansell had again snatched pole, took the lead from Senna (second on the grid) on lap two, and then diced with Prost (who took over a few laps later) before retaking the lead for a few more laps. After the pair had made their tyre stops Prost was ahead again and Mansell was fighting back hard, when his engine seized and he pulled up on the stadium infield.

In the closing stages only Piquet and Johansson's McLaren were on the same lap. But the drama was not yet over. A race which brought so many mechanical disasters, with only seven cars running at the finish (and one of those too far behind to be classified) ended spectacularly.

As he came into the stadium for the last time Johansson's right front tyre, which had been slowly deflating, let go completely. With the tyre in tatters he wrestled his McLaren three-wheeler painfully around the final bends, and just managed to limp home for second place.

Although he was second quickest in qualifying, and led the opening lap, Senna's Lotus could make only token resistance and he was lucky to pick up third place after a catalogue of disasters. He lost his cockpit turbo-boost control, had to stop to replace a damaged nose wing, and struggled with his car's handling when his active suspension failed after a leak in the hydraulics.

Hockenheim is a power circuit and before the

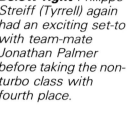

Below right Philippe Streiff (Tyrrell) again had an exciting set-to with team-mate Jonathan Palmer before taking the non-turbo class with fourth place.

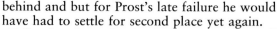

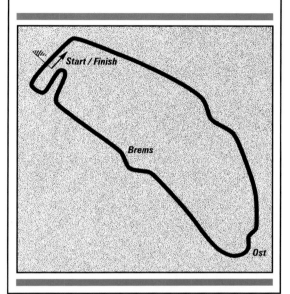

GERMAN GRAND PRIX
— 26 July —

44 laps, 185.8 miles

The Hockenheimring is fast and flat, and would be faster still but for the three chicanes. Most spectators are confined to the 'stadium' area, where overtaking is difficult.

race the superior power of the turbos had overwhelmed the 3.5-litre machines, with the fastest 'atmospheric' no less than 10 seconds behind poleman in qualifying. The sages nodded their heads and gave the normally aspirated cars no chance. How wrong they were. With all but one of the 21 turbo cars in some sort of trouble, the less powerful cars had a field day.

Philippe Alliot led the non-turbo battle initially in his Lola but had to give way to the Tyrrell twins, who took it in turns to lead this race within a race. Palmer and Streiff gave the spectators plenty of excitement as they battled it out wheel to wheel. Then Palmer slid on oil, letting Streiff through, and at that point Ken Tyrrell decided it was prudent to signal his drivers to hold position rather than continue to fight and maybe put themselves off the track.

So it was Streiff fourth and Palmer (not too happy about the instruction to stay behind) fifth, and Alliot sixth: three 3.5-litre cars in the points on a circuit where few would have given odds on them getting any points at all.

Meanwhile, behind the scenes, Senna was not the happiest of drivers. He was becoming less enamoured of the sophisticated Lotus suspension. He was, in fact, looking for another team; and his decision to leave Lotus at season's end came shortly afterwards.

Eight races gone, eight to come, and the points table read: Piquet 39, Senna 35, Mansell 30, Prost 26. A lot of points were yet to be won and the championship race was wide open.

Above *Philippe Alliot (Lola) gave the emergent Larrousse team renewed hope by leading the non-turbo class until forced back into sixth place.*

Left *Nigel Mansell (left, going wide at a corner) and Nelson Piquet contested the middle section of the race with leader Alain Prost after they had fitted fresh rubber. But only Piquet made it to the finish.*

1	Nelson Piquet (Williams-Honda FW11B)	1h 21m 25.091s, 136.946mph
2	Stefan Johansson (McLaren-TAG MP4/3)	1h 23m 04.682s
3	Ayrton Senna (Lotus-Honda 99T)	1 lap down
4	Philippe Streiff (Tyrrell-Cosworth DG/016)	1 lap down
5	Jonathan Palmer (Tyrrell-Cosworth DG/016)	1 lap down
6	Philippe Alliot (Lola-Cosworth LC87)	2 laps down

Fastest lap *Mansell, 1m 45.716s, 143.823mph (record for revised circuit)*

NELSON IN LUCK AGAIN

Warwick Shows True Grit

Racing drivers, whatever the result of their last race, always have their eyes firmly fixed on the next; history plays little part in their thinking. But Mansell must have recalled, however fleetingly, that in 1986 he won the French and British GPs and then lost out to Piquet in the next two in Germany and Hungary.

In fact history, with uncharacteristic neatness, was to repeat itself in 1987: two wins for Mansell in France and Britain, then two on the trot for Piquet. And yet again Britain's top driver felt he had been robbed by circumstances beyond his control. In Monaco, Detroit and Hockenheim he had led only to see his hopes dashed, and the gremlins struck again at the Hungaroring. This time it was the more galling

because his retirement was both late in the race and caused by a problem which had never previously hit the Williams team.

Mansell was in good spirits on race eve. He had celebrated his 33rd birthday by grabbing yet another number one spot on the grid; and he knew that Piquet would not be the thorn in his Williams effort the following year. Frank Williams had got the news from Piquet the day before first practice. When Senna had indicated that he did not want to continue with Lotus in 1988, Team Lotus director Peter Warr had acted promptly to snap up Piquet as replacement. But that did not mean Piquet would relax in his effort to take his third world championship in 1987.

Above Everyone suffered from lack of grip on the slippery Hungaroring – none more so than Ayrton Senna, whose Lotus was also plagued by vibrations and gearbox trouble. But he hung on to take second place.

Left Nelson Piquet (seen here taking a dry line during qualifying) won his second GP in succession – but only because Nigel Mansell's Williams shed a rear-wheel nut after he had led for 70 of the 76 laps.

HUNGARIAN GRAND PRIX

9 August

76 laps, 189.5 miles

The Hungaroring, opened in 1986, staged the first GP behind the Iron Curtain. In a splendid setting a few miles out of Budapest, with good facilities; some drivers complain it is too slow.

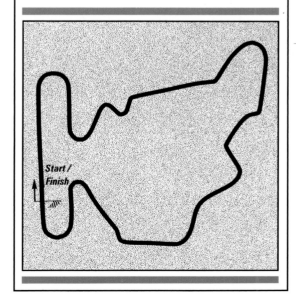

Start / Finish

There was also a new threat on the grid at the Hungaroring, which was staging its second Grand Prix and again attracting huge crowds. The Ferrari team, under stronger discipline from new technical director John Barnard, seemed to be getting its act together at last. Gerhard Berger was alongside Mansell on the grid, ahead of Piquet and Prost, with Alboreto underlining the team's potential on the third row. It was the first time we had seen a Ferrari on the front row since the German GP at the new Nürburgring two years earlier.

Was this to be the Ferrari comeback, long overdue and eagerly awaited? The early race laps suggested it could be, with Berger, although weak from 'flu, snapping at Mansell's heels and Alboreto lying third. But after 13 laps Berger fell victim to a failed differential and it was left to Alboreto to sustain the challenge.

Mansell was able to hold off the remaining Ferrari fairly comfortably, and Alboreto was releated to third place when Piquet swooped past him on lap 29. Alboreto lay third for a further 14 laps before his engine died. Glum faces in the Ferrari camp; the cars were becoming more competitive but they had failed to pick up a single point in four successive races. The search for reliability had to be redoubled.

Meanwhile, a vibration problem was troubling Piquet and there was no way he could get on to terms with Mansell, provided his team-mate's car stayed healthy.

If Mansell won with Piquet second, the latter's

Right Gerhard Berger (Ferrari) spins during practice as Pascal Fabre's AGS-Ford (centre) and Derek Warwick's Arrows storm past. Fabre lasted only one lap in the race, and Berger only 13; but Warwick, fighting off flu, took a splendid sixth place, in the points for the second time in 1987.

points lead over Mansell would be reduced to a manageable six. With six laps to go the small but vociferous British element in the crowd were waving Union Jacks and preparing to celebrate.

Then came disaster. Mansell suddenly slowed. Had his engine seized again, as in Germany? No: this time the right rear wheel nut had worked loose and flown off. A TV camera homed in on a sad Mansell, sitting on a barrier by his stricken car, wondering why he had to be so unlucky and watching his team-mate repeat his 1986 victory behind the Iron Curtain.

Senna was another driver bedevilled by a vibration problem which left him exhausted; but he struggled on in spite of a bruised back and lack of track grip to take second place. Derek Warwick's physical problems had begun before the race. During practice he had been trying to throw off the effects of a bout of 'flu aggravated by conjunctivitus in one eye. He was not sure he would be able to complete the race; but finish he did, in sixth place − a really heroic effort that included recovering from being rammed by his Arrows team-mate, Eddie Cheever. Brave Warwick had to be lifted from the cockpit when the race ended.

The McLaren team had fitted a new type of alternator drive-belt to overcome the problem which had hit them in previous races, but Prost suffered from an intermittent misfire and felt fortunate to finish third, while Johansson fell out after only 14 laps when his transmission seized (in spinning he nearly put Prost off the track).

The Benettons had looked promising in practice. And, though Teo Fabi was soon out with gearbox trouble, Boutsen gave Senna a tremendous fight for several laps. But the Belgian driver found his brakes losing their potency and dropped back further when he lost boost pressure, to finish fourth, a lap behind the leaders.

The Brabham team had so far endured a disappointing year, but there was some cheer for them when Riccardo Patrese finished fifth for his first points of the season.

The 3.5-litre battle began again went to Palmer, who finished seventh overall. It was Palmer's fifth win in his class and he now had a handy 12-points lead over fellow Tyrrell driver Streiff.

Mansell later did his best to look cheerful after his wretched luck but he was no less than 18 points behind Piquet. It would need good fortune as well as all his skill and fightng qualities to close that gap.

1 Nelson Piquet (Williams-Honda FW11B)		1h 59m 26.793s, 95.218mph
2 Ayrton Senna (Lotus-Honda 99T)		2h 00m 04.520s
3 Alain Prost (McLaren-TAG MP4/3)		2h 00m 54.520s
4 Thierry Boutsen (Benetton-Ford B187)		1 lap down
5 Riccardo Patrese (Brabham-BMW BT56)		1 lap down
6 Derek Warwick (Arrows-Megatron A10)		2 laps down

Fastest lap *Piquet, 1m 30.149s, 99.602mph (record)*

Above Alain Prost managed to salvage something from the Hungaroring. His car, misfiring from the start, was never in serious contention — but he coaxed it patiently into third place.

LET'S START AGAIN — AND AGAIN!

Mansell Makes It Through the Chaos

This was Mansell's 100th grand prix. His first had been at the same track in 1980, a painful debut when fuel leaked into his Lotus cockpit and burned his skin. This time, trouble began before the meeting opened. In agony from an abscess, he had a wisdom tooth removed the night before practice and had to struggle along on a diet of pain-killers.

The capricious Österreichring weather effectively washed out final qualifying and by then Piquet was established on pole, with Mansell fractionally slower: the fourth all-Williams front row of the year.

On the first day Stefan Johansson had walked back to his pits after practice and admitted he had been badly scared. Cresting the brow of a hill at over 150 mph, he was confronted by a deer bounding across the track. He swerved, but his McLaren hit the unfortunate animal; and Johansson's machine was further damaged when he slammed into a barrier. Johansson was

Below left *During practice Stefan Johansson crashed into a stray deer that cantered onto the track. Badly bruised, he started the race in the spare car.*

Below *The carnage at Österreichring continued with the now-habitual startline pile-up. This one featured Piercarlo Ghinzani's Ligier (left), Prost's McLaren (centre, rear), Pascal Fabre's AGS (centre), Philippe Alliot's Lola (right) and others after Martin Brundle's Zakspeed had bounced off the left-side guardrail.*

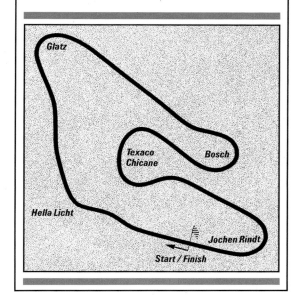

AUSTRIAN GRAND PRIX
— 16 August —

52 laps, 191.9 miles

The Österreichring vies with Silverstone as the fastest circuit in the F1 calendar. Its straights and sweeping curves call for courage and skill.

not only frightened but furious: some time before the deer had been seen running around close to the track, but officials had not seen fit to halt practice.

On a hot and sunny Sunday afternoon the race began; but almost at once Martin Brundle's Zakspeed snapped left, rammed the guardrail and bounced back across the track. The result was a series of collisions involving half a dozen cars.

With the track blocked the race was halted, to be restarted 40 minutes later, with some drivers in repaired cars, others in spares. This time there was even more chaos. Mansell, with a slipping clutch, could only crawl away and drivers behind him got into all sorts of trouble as they took avoiding action. Nearly half the grid was involved in the mêlée, with bits flying in all directions; again, mercifully, no-one was injured.

The cars lined up once more nearly two hours later. Frantic work by mechanics enabled 25 cars to get away, only Streiff a non-starter with both his race cars and the spare Tyrrell too badly damaged. For various reasons six drivers started from the pit lane, among them Alboreto and Prost.

Third time lucky. The field got away safely,

though Senna caused further anxiety by stalling on the line. On race eve, Piquet had admitted he would be quite content to finish second and just pick up points, but he led from the grid, chased by Boutsen, whose Benetton was handling beautifully on the fast curves. Berger lay third for three laps before slipping back two places and then retiring with a blown turbo, to the intense disappointment of his home crowd.

Boutsen continued to challenge Piquet with Mansell, who had started cautiously to nurse his clutch, lying third after Berger's retirement. But Boutsen's effort was thwarted when he had to pit

to have his gear linkage fixed.

Mansell was now second, hard on Piquet's heels and trying to harry him into error. His chance came on lap 21 as they came upon a back-marker. As Piquet hesitated momentarily Mansell made a bold bid and was through. Piquet several times tried to counter-attack but to no avail and Mansell held his lead right through to the finish.

Despite having to make two stops for fresh tyres – he missed his pit the first time and had to go round the circuit again – Fabi took third place, while Boutsen, who had further trouble

Above *Nigel Mansell had plenty to smile about, outwitting rival Nelson Piquet when both were forcing their way through slower traffic on lap 21, and going on to win by almost a minute.*

with a loose undertray, was fourth. Alboreto joined Berger in the dead-car park after an exhaust broke. That followed a stern battle with Senna during which they touched, causing Senna to make a hurried visit to the pits to have a replacement nose. Prost's engine lost power just when it seemed he would take third place, and he dropped back to finish sixth, behind Senna.

It was Ivan Capelli's turn to win the normally aspirated battle, with Palmer unable to make any impression because of a broken valve-spring. But Palmer took another four points for the Jim Clark Cup and now led Streiff by 16 points.

The race ended on a farcical note when the man with the chequered flag missed Mansell when he had completed the full 52 laps. This was not the end of a day of mistakes and mishaps. As Mansell was driven in a jeep back to the rostrum he turned sideways to pass his helmet down to a colleague and banged his head hard into a gantry. Fabi poured a bottle of water over the stricken Mansell to bring him round. In spite of a hole in his jaw and a growing bump on his forehead, Mansell declared himself feeling fine. There's nothing like winning to make a driver forget such trivial distractions.

1	Nigel Mansell (Williams-Honda FW11B)	1h 18m 44.898s, 146.283mph
2	Nelson Piquet (Williams-Honda FW11B)	1h 19m 40.602s
3	Teo Fabi (Benetton-Ford B187)	1 lap down
4	Thierry Boutsen (Benetton-Ford B187)	1 lap down
5	Ayrton Senna (Lotus-Honda 99T)	2 laps down
6	Alain Prost (McLaren-TAG MP4/3)	2 laps down

Fastest lap *Mansell, 1m 28.318s, 150.5mph (record)*

A CLASSIC PIQUET-SENNA DUEL

Williams 'Reactive' Earns Its Colours

Below *Nelson Piquet just managed to hold off Ayrton Senna in a race dominated by cars with computer-controlled suspensions. Senna's Lotus was well-developed by now, but it was a first* outing for the 'reactive' system on the Williams.

Less than two hours after the Williams duo had set the pace in the first qualifying session, Honda, with coldly impeccable timing, staged a press conference in the Monza park to tell the world they were ditching the team in 1988 and switching their engines to McLaren.

The inscrutable boss of Honda's F1 effort fielded searching media questions with impassive calm but his answers failed to satisfy the many who wondered why, after all the Williams team had done for them – 20 wins to date – the Japanese firm was stopping the supply of engines at the end of the season, even though the contract was due to continue for another year.

Although Yoshitoshi Sakurai insisted that the break with Williams was 'mutual' and spoke of the need for 'new challenges', it was not a convincing performance. The consensus was that Frank Williams had shown too much independence in running his team, had refused to accept Nakajima on the driving strength (as Lotus had done), and had been too even-handed in his treatment of his drivers, whereas Honda had wanted Nelson Piquet to be the undisputed star. Not only were McLaren to get Honda engines to replace their ageing TAG units: the team also announced the signing of Senna to partner Prost in 1988.

ITALIAN GRAND PRIX
— 6 September —

50 laps, 180.2 miles
Set in a former royal park a few miles north of Milan, the Monza track has a long and rich history. Slower since the insertion of three chicanes on safety grounds.

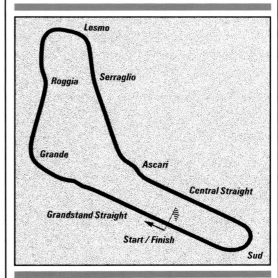

In his bid to increase his championship lead Piquet had Williams' new 'secret weapon' at Monza. During the season he had carried out intensive testing of the team's active suspension system. With bad memories of frightening episodes years earlier with the fist version of the Lotus active system, Mansell had shied away from driving the experimental Williams. Now it looked as though he might have made a mistake. Piquet's car was clearly quicker than Mansell's in a straight line. Running closer to the track surface with better ground effect it was able to carry less rear wing. Still, Mansell was only just a little slower than Piquet in the front row line-up and the Ferrari fans were delirious to see Berger in third spot.

The start had to be aborted when Patrese's Brabham spewed flames. Nothing serious: the fire was soon put out, and after another parade lap the race began, to be run over one lap less than originally scheduled. Mansell led initially but Piquet pipped him into the first chicane. While Piquet sped on Mansell was suddenly relegated to fourth on lap two, headed by Boutsen's Benetton and Berger (with whom he banged wheels at the second chicane).

Mansell put on the pressure and was briefly lying second before stopping for tyres. When the flurry of tyre changes was over it was Senna who led from Piquet.

But Senna had yet to make his stop . . . or so everyone thought. Senna had other ideas. Having won in Detroit without stopping for fresh rubber, he radioed the Lotus pit and inquired how his rivals' tyres had looked when they made their change. Was there, he asked, any chance of continuing to the finish? Lotus conferred with Goodyear and the answer came back: Yes, it might *just* be possible.

Meanwhile, Piquet was cutting into Senna's advantage, though the effort was blistering his new tyres and bringing a vibration. Senna was using all his cunning to conserve his tyres but he knew it would be hard to hold his lead. In a desperate effort to gain an advantage in the traffic, he tried to overtake Ghinzani's Ligier on the inside going into the big sweeping right-hander at the end of the back straight. Unfortunately there was less grip on that inside line; he lost control and rushed into the sand run-off on the outside of the curve. He kept his engine going and got back on to the track, but Piquet had slipped through to retake the lead.

Despite his ailing tyres Senna drove right on the limit. It became a great duel. Piquet set a new lap record and Senna beat that on the penultimate lap — but Piquet got home by less than two seconds. Mansell had to settle for a somewhat distant third, handicapped by his engine overheating owing to debris caught up in his radiator air intakes (it seemed, in retrospect, remarkable

that, as in Brazil the intakes were not fitted with grilles to prevent this happening).

Berger salved some Ferrari pride by grabbing fourth place from Boutsen after the Benetton's undertray came loose (the Belgian was further worried by his fuel consumption). Alboreto's hopes of celebrating his 100th GP outing before his doting fans were dashed early on when he ran over a kerb, lost part of the Ferrari bodywork and overheated the turbo. Prost had a troubled race, his McLaren plagued by his engine cutting out intermittently. His chances of retaining the world title now looked remote. The remaining point went to Johansson, who drove doggedly despite various mechanical ailments, his ribs strapped after that confrontation with the deer in Austria, and the knowledge that he would have to look for another berth in 1988.

Five championship rounds to go: Piquet 14 points ahead of Senna, and Mansell 20 in arrears. It would demand a superhuman effort plus more than a touch of luck for Mansell to catch Piquet now.

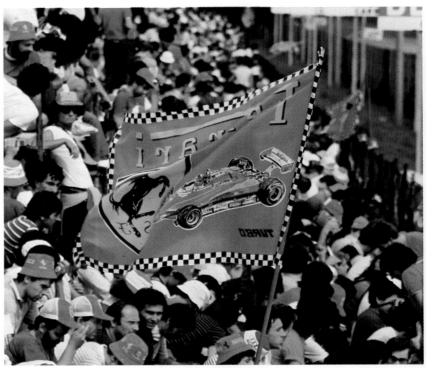

Above Italian fans at Monza presented a noisy and colourful lobby on behalf of the Prancing Horse.

Right Senna, on original rubber throughout, led comfortably with only seven laps to go. But his worn tyres caused him to skid while overtaking Ghinzani's Ligier, and Piquet shot past him.

1 Nelson Piquet (Williams-Honda FW11B)		1h 14m 47.707s, 144.553mph
2 Ayrton Senna (Lotus-Honda 99T)		1h 14m 49.513s
3 Nigel Mansell (Williams-Honda FW11B)		1h 15m 36.743s
4 Gerhard Berger (Ferrari F1/87)		1h 15m 45.686s
5 Thierry Boutsen (Benetton-Ford B187)		1h 16m 09.026s
6 Stefan Johansson (McLaren-TAG MP4/3)		1h 16m 16.494s

Fastest lap *Senna, 1m 26.796s, 149.479mph (record)*

PROST BEATS THE FIELD (AND JACKIE STEWART)

Ferrari Put Down a Marker

Although they had achieved, by their standards, only very modest results during the first half of the season, the Ferrari team were slowly feeling their way to the sort of competitiveness expected of them.

Under the perfectionist authority of technical director John Barnard, plus the expertise of designer Harvey Postlethwaite working in the new Ferrari wind-tunnel, the red cars were gradually being honed to challenge the front-runners. Only unreliability was preventing them from finishing well in the points.

The race at Estoril marked a turning point in Ferrari fortunes. Berger (helped, it is true, by choosing a brief moment for qualifying when the

track was dry) had a Ferrari on pole for the first time since Brazil in April 1985. It was also a first-time pole for Berger, and with Alboreto on the third row but looking confident, many sensed this could be the time when the prancing horse galloped again.

The Williams team turned up with four machines, two each for Piquet and Mansell. Like Piquet, Mansell had the option of a car with active suspension (after the Italian race he had tested an active car at Brands Hatch and convinced himself it offered an advantage). After qualifying both drivers opted to 'go active'.

Since the first GP at Estoril there had been three memorable races. Prost won in 1984, but had

Below Alain Prost (McLaren) acknowledges the marshals' flags at Estoril on breaking Jackie Stewart's 14-year-old record of 27 grand prix victories.

PORTUGUESE GRAND PRIX
— 20 September —

70 laps, 189.2 miles

Estoril circuit, set in the hills a few miles from the seaside resort west of Lisbon, staged its first GP in 1984. An interesting mixture of long straight, fast and slow corners. Liked by most drivers.

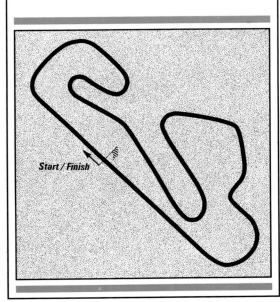

Start / Finish

Above Teo Fabi elected to run non-stop – then overtaxed his tyres when trying to pass Nelson Piquet to take the lead. On the last lap he dropped back to fourth spot as his fuel ran out.

lost the world title to team-mate Lauda by just half a point. Senna won his first GP in 1985 after a magical display of wet-weather driving. And in 1986 Mansell simply pulverised the opposition with his finest performance of the year.

Another race for the history books in 1987? Yes – but hardly in line with experts' predictions.

For the third GP in succession there was an aborted start. Going into the first corner Piquet and Alboreto made contact and the inevitable shambles resulted. What followed was an appalling example of official incompetence. With the track blocked the red flag should have gone out at the start-finish line, but the official reaction was too slow and the pack, headed by Berger and Mansell, roared into lap two, approached the stricken cars at high speed and avoided disaster

by a hairsbreadth. Then the red flag went up.

Several drivers took over spare cars for the restart and Piquet's mechanics repaired his Williams just in time for the reformed grid. Mansell made his usual rapid getaway but had correctly forecast that he would soon be taken down the straight because his engine did not feel one hundred per cent. Sure enough, Berger sailed past on lap two and began to pull away. Mansell counter-attacked but on lap 14 the Williams suddenly slowed, running on less than six cylinders, and came to a halt out on the circuit.

That let Piquet into second place. Berger was storming along in front and before half distance Alboreto took Piquet to make it a Ferrari one–two – something not seen for quite a time.

Alboreto led for a couple of laps after Berger

stopped for tyres but Berger took over again and soon after the Italian retired with gearbox trouble – Ferrari fragility again. Could Berger keep going? He had now come under pressure from Fabi, who had opted to run his Benetton through on one set of tyres. Fabi later faded, finishing fourth, a lap behind and out of fuel, but Berger's real challenge was slowly mounting from Prost, whose McLaren had suffered from a vibration earlier on but now felt fine on fresh tyres. The Frenchman was at his superb best, gradually chipping away at Berger's lead and doing so with disarming smoothness. Berger's second set of tyres were losing their edge, but he was fighting tooth and nail to keep the lead. He responded to the Prof's threat by going yet faster, but Prost hunted him remorselessly. With

Left *Stefan Johansson lost much of Saturday's practice while mechanics worked on his misfiring engine. In the race he pulled up from eighth place to finish fifth.*

Above *Gerhard Berger took pole position at Estoril and had nearly won the race until relentless hounding by Prost caused him to spin with three laps to go.*

He still finished in second place, breaking the circuit record on lap 66.

10 laps to go the McLaren was less than four seconds behind, and closing. Five laps later the margin was only 2½ seconds. Berger set a new lap record on lap 66 but Prost was still in his mirrors, trying to force the Austrian into an indiscretion.

It happened with less than three laps to go. Under intense pressure, Berger made a small but crucial error going into a right-hander, spun – and Prost was through in an instant. Berger managed to get away again, but he had no hope of catching Prost, who went on to log his 28th GP victory – and crack Jackie Stewart's record dating back to 1973. A rueful Berger crossed the line some 20 seconds behind and admitted that on his worn tyres he simply could not resist Prost's determined challenge.

It was a magnificent drive by Prost, a demonstration that given a healthy car he could usually show he was the master. Jackie Stewart commented: 'There is no doubt that Alain is head and shoulders above all current grand-prix drivers.... I can't think of anybody I would rather have taken my record.'

Piquet had to be content with third place this time (his lowest position in 10 scoring races) after struggling with oversteer when his Williams undertray worked loose. Once again Johansson had shown real grit, coping with a wobbling front wheel but still getting his McLaren into fifth place. Eddie Cheever (Arrows) snatched sixth place, ahead of Senna, who had lost three laps early on while an electronic fault was remedied, and then drove splendidly to pull back from last.

A tremendous race, a magnificent result for Prost, and the promise that Ferrari were at last on the way back.

1	Alain Prost (McLaren-TAG MP4/3)	1h 37m 03.906s, 116.957mph
2	Gerhard Berger (Ferrari F1/87)	1h 37m 24.399s
3	Nelson Piquet (Williams-Honda FW11B)	1h 38m 07.210s
4	Teo Fabi (Benetton-Ford B187)	1 lap down
5	Stefan Johansson (McLaren-TAG MP4/3)	1 lap down
6	Eddie Cheever (Arrows-Megatron A10)	2 laps down

Fastest lap *Berger, 1m 19.282s, 122.737mph (record)*

WILLIAMS CLINCH CONSTRUCTORS' TITLE

Senna Holds Up the Traffic

The brand-new Jerez circuit, in the heart of the sherry region, staged an exciting first GP in 1986, when Mansell's pursuit of Senna failed at the line by just 14 hundredths of a second. In 1987, Mansell made no mistake. With a drive of consummate skill and impeccable control he snatched the lead from Piquet at the end of the opening lap and roared on to his fifth win of the season.

Senna could not provide any real threat this time, but his strategy of driving through without a pit stop (as he had done in 1986) brought a situation in which he was chased for lap after lap by a whole gaggle of frustrated drivers, some of whom were able to overtake only when the Lotus's tyres deteriorated badly in the closing laps. Senna eventually finished fifth, after holding second place with 10 laps to go.

Whatever the reason (and it could have been annoyance at being bested by Mansell, who was driving a less-competitive car), Piquet's race was, on his own admission, more packed with errors than in any other GP in 1987. He spun his Williams to lose two places and later misjudged a corner, ran too wide and lost places again. But his biggest mistake came earlier, during his tyre stop, when he failed to hit the brake pedal as the car was on its jacks, and for a few frantic seconds his mechanics could not work on spinning rear wheels.

Whereas Mansell was at rest in the pits for just over 11 seconds (by no means a fast change) Piquet's time was eight seconds more – a lifetime in GP terms. He finished fourth.

Mansell's commanding drive surely stemmed in part from a strong feeling that he had been sandbagged by his team-mate during qualifying. Both Williams drivers had available a 'passive' and an 'active' machine. Unconvinced by the 'active's' reliability and still not fully confident in it Mansell concentrated on the car he knew better. That confidence seemed justified when, towards the end of final qualifying, he looked destined for his eighth pole of the year. But Piquet went out late and knocked a big chunk off Mansell's time, demonstrating – so Mansell thought – that the Brazilian had duped him. Learning he had been outwitted, Mansell rushed into the pit lane and failed to observe the signal

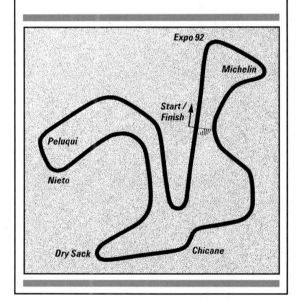

to have his car weighed. Anxious to get into his 'active' car, Mansell jumped out and ran to his pits to put in a couple of laps. For breaking the rules he was fined, his final session times were disallowed, and he had second spot on the grid.

The Senna decision to drive through on one set of tyres involved setting up his car to be fast down the straights but less speedy round the corners. But the Jerez circuit is tight, with few overtaking opportunities – which is why Senna was able to hold off all challenges until his tyres lost their edge.

Behind Senna were the two Ferraris, both Benettons and Prost's McLaren. Berger attacked first, then Alboreto made an effort. With frustration boiling over, Berger later tried to snatch a

Right Riccardo Patrese (Brabham) with lack of tyre grip, takes to the country; Eddie Cheever (Arrows) speeds by to finish eighth.

Below In one of his most commanding performances, Mansell thrust aside Nelson Piquet's challenge on lap 1 and was a comfortable 22 seconds ahead of Alain Prost at the chequered flag.

Right *Ayrton Senna, fifth on the grid, made a superb start at Jerez, resisting all attempts by Prost and Alboreto (seen here), then Boutsen, Berger and Piquet, to overtake his ill-handling Lotus. Then his tyres – the original set – lost their grip and he swiftly dropped to fifth place.*

place from Alboreto and Prost seized his opportunity to overtake both in one brilliantly incisive manoeuvre.

That put Prost up to fourth, then third as he took Piquet. Still the switching of positions went on in this thrilling tussle. Boutsen forced his Benetton into third on two occasions and seemed set for second place as he hounded Senna, but the Belgian's brakes faded and he spun off. This was yet another race where the handsome Benettons had promised much but fell victim to mechanical malaise: Fabi, too, had been going strongly but retired with engine trouble.

Both Ferraris also failed. Berger ran over a kerb, smashed an oil cooler and retired 10 laps from the finish. Alboreto, who made a tremendous effort to pinch Senna's place (the two drivers are *not* the best of friends), retired with an expired engine when lying fourth with five laps to go.

With Piquet in late trouble and making a quick stop to have debris removed from his car, the patient and methodical Prost took over second place, far behind Mansell but well satisfied since the Williams clearly had the heels of all the opposition at Jerez. Driving the other McLaren, Johansson also got past Piquet in the dying laps to take third place.

Further down the field there were, as so often, some splendid battles in the non-turbo class. Palmer in his Tyrrell and Alliot for Lola fought strongly for supremacy, with the Englishman just holding the Frenchman at bay. But on lap 55 the pair came upon Arnoux in his Ligier. Not for nothing is Arnoux often described as a mobile chicane: he has been involved in many incidents over the years, and this was another. As Palmer came alongside to overtake, Arnoux turned into his path. The luckless Palmer was booted off the track and into retirement, robbed through no fault of his own of his sixth class win of the season.

Alliot went on to win the class and also picked up a championship point by placing sixth overall. Streiff was just behind and closed to within seven points of Palmer in the Jim Clark Cup competition.

Mansell's continuing vendetta with Piquet was echoed in the rivalry of the two Tyrrell drivers, each determined to win the Jim Clark Cup. But the inter-Tyrrell struggle was on a sporting basis, far removed from the heat in the Williams team.

1	Nigel Mansell (Williams-Honda FW11B)	1h 49m 12.692s, 103.674mph
2	Alain Prost (McLaren-TAG MP4/3)	1h 49m 34.917s
3	Stefan Johansson (McLaren-TAG MP4/3)	1h 49m 43.510s
4	Nelson Piquet (Williams-Honda FW11B)	1h 49m 44.142s
5	Ayrton Senna (Lotus-Honda 99T)	1h 50m 26.199s
6	Philippe Alliot (Lola-Cosworth LC87)	1 lap down

Fastest lap *Gerhard Berger (Ferrari F1/87), 1m 26.986s, 108.470mph (record)*

MANSELL MAKES IT SIX

A Race of Two Halves

Above The drivers condemned the bumpy Mexican circuit, whose condition led to many accidents. Derek Warwick's Arrows, seen here, crashed after his suspension could take no more on lap 26.

Mexico City, at over 7,000 feet, is far away the highest venue in the Formula 1 calendar; but the 1987 race, the second to be held on the revised Autodromo Hermanos Rodriguez, was a messy affair which failed to reach the heights.

It did, however, halve the number of championship contenders: Prost and Senna went out of the chase, and with two rounds to go only Piquet and Mansell were left to fight it out. There was also controversy, questions being raised as to whether Piquet should have been disqualified for getting a push-start after colliding with Prost on the first lap. But it was deemed to be in order, since it served to move Piquet from a potentially dangerous position on the circuit.

Both Senna and Mansell were in trouble during qualifying, flying off the road at the very rapid, slightly banked sweep leading to the pits straight. Fortunately, neither was injured, a tribute to the sturdiness and impact-cushioning of modern grand prix cars. Despite his alarming experience Mansell was again on pole, for the eighth time in the season, and he set a record by being on the front row for 15 successive GPs. Berger again demonstrated Ferrari's growing potential by setting second fastest time.

Though improvements had been made to the circuit it was still extremely bumpy and also tough on tyres. Goodyear pushed up the normal allocation of tyres from 10 per car to 15, giving a choice between a softer and a harder type. Piquet – significantly – chose the harder rubber.

63 laps, 173.1 miles

This circuit, a few miles from the centre of sprawling Mexico City, was refurbished for the 1986 GP and renamed after the two Rodriguez brothers who died in racing accidents. Over 7,000 feet above sea level.

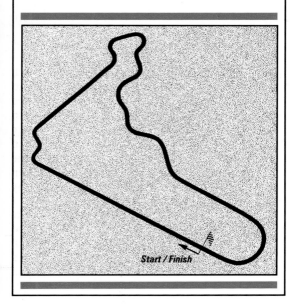

Start / Finish

Mansell was slow away at the start, scrabbling for grip on the slippier side of the track, and was immediately passed by Berger, Boutsen, Piquet and Prost. The Prost–Piquet coming together removed Prost from the action immediately; but after marshals had got him going again, Piquet began a splendid chase from the back of the field.

Revelling in the Benetton's handling (Berger had won in a Benetton the year before), Boutsen stormed past Berger on lap two and found himself leading for the first time in his grand prix career. He led convincingly until lap 15, when he retired yet again, this time with an electronic problem. Berger took over but his glory was short-lived; seven laps later he, too, was side-lined with a blown engine.

Now Mansell was leading, ahead of Senna and an inspired Riccardo Patrese, whose Brabham was showing unexpected form. Prost was not the only driver out early. Nakajima had brain fade on lap two, rammed Warwick's Arrows, and caused Johansson (McLaren) and Danner (Zakspeed) to clash and retire on the spot. An understandably annoyed Warwick pitted for replacement parts and went out again, but the bump from Nakajima could well have weakened a component and may have led to a massive high-speed accident after 31 laps, when he slid off at the notorious final bend, thudded into a tyre wall and was fortunate to be no more than shocked.

The race was stopped while the tyre wall was rebuilt and positions for the 33-lap restart

Above Nelson Piquet gained few Brownie points when his Williams spun and made a mess of Prost's McLaren on lap 1. Piquet was lucky to avoid disqualification for a push re-start.

decided by the placings at 30 laps. Piquet was not pleased that his rivals were able to fit new tyres without the disadvantage of a pit stop. The new grid, cut by the accidents and retirements to 15, was headed by Mansell, followed by Senna, Patrese and Piquet, who had driven like the wind to haul himself up to fourth.

The race result would be decided on aggregate and Mansell felt comfortable because he had finished the first 'heat' some 45 seconds ahead of Piquet. But Piquet was determined to claw back the advantage if he could. He led and fought off two determined efforts by Mansell, who then settled for keeping Piquet in his sights, knowing he had that time cushion from the first 'heat'.

Piquet took third place on aggregate from Patrese, and then second from Senna, who had lost his clutch and in missing a gear spun and stalled his engine. Thinking he would be push-

started as Piquet had been, Senna was furious when marshals pushed him with little urgency and suggested he should pull off up an escape road. He leapt out of his Lotus and was later fined heavily for striking a marshal. So Senna followed Prost with DNF ('did not finish') against his name, and now neither had championship hopes.

Piquet came home first in the second 'heat', but Mansell had played it shrewdly and on aggregate won his sixth GP of the year, with Piquet second. Patrese, who had recently been confirmed as Mansell's partner for 1988, celebrated with third, with Cheever fourth for Arrows and Fabi fifth in the other Benetton.

Alliot had the legs of the two Tyrrells in the 'second division' battle and picked up a championship point by finishing sixth but Palmer, who finished seventh, ahead of Streiff, increased his

Left Nigel Mansell (seen lapping the Ligiers of René Arnoux and Piercarlo Ghinzani) won both halves of a race re-started after Warwick's crash.

Above Riccardo Patrese (Brabham) sweeps past Gerhard Berger as the Ferrari's turbo fails on the 21st lap. Patrese went on to take third place.

1 Nigel Mansell (Williams-Honda FW11B)	1h 26m 24.207s, 120.179mph	
2 Nelson Piquet (Williams-Honda FW11B)	1h 26m 50.383s	
3 Riccardo Patrese (Brabham-BMW BT56)	1h 27m 51.086s	
4 Eddie Cheever (Arrows-Megatron A10)	1h 28m 05.559s	
5 Teo Fabi (Benetton-Ford B187)	2 laps down	
6 Philippe Alliot (Lola-Cosworth LC87)	3 laps down	

Fastest lap *Piquet, 1m 19.132s, 124.974mph (record)*

Jim Clark Cup lead to nine points over his team-mate.

Now, with two rounds to go, it was certain that one of the Williams drivers would be crowned champion. No-one could catch them. The points score was Piquet 73, Mansell 61, a 12-point gap, but not without hope for Mansell since Piquet had scored in 12 rounds and was already having to discard points (since only a driver's best 11 results could count). The chips were down and the Japanese GP two weeks hence had all the makings of a terrific contest. The odds favoured Piquet but Mansell would be doing his utmost to buck them.

FORZA FERRARI!

Mansell's Shunt Gives Piquet the Title

The first Japanese GP, in 1976, run at the Mount Fuji circuit, had seen James Hunt clinch the drivers' world championship. Eleven years later the title was again wrapped up in Japan. But this time it was decided two days *before* the race when Mansell, trying to snatch provisional pole from Piquet in the first qualifying session, went off the tarmac at high speed and was injured so badly that he could take no further part. In considerable pain, he was flown home to the Isle of Man. It would be more than three months before he was fit enough to be back in a Williams cockpit.

With the Mansell threat removed, Piquet became champion for the third time, adding to titles won in 1981 and 1983. Even Piquet, despite the enmity between him and Mansell, conceded it was not the way he would have wished to become champion again.

The 1987 race was run on the Suzuka circuit, owned by Honda and used by them for testing. It was designed by Dutchman John Hugenholtz (who was responsible for the Zandvoort track) and features a crossover involving a bidge and

JAPANESE GRAND PRIX
— 1 November —

51 laps, 185.7 miles

The Suzuka circuit, officially opened a quarter of a century earlier, staged its first GP in 1987. Unusual in incorporating a crossover and a tunnel.

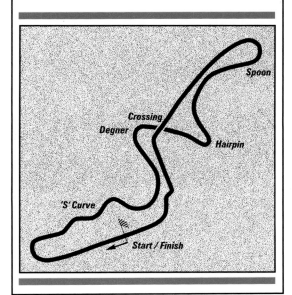

Left Nigel Mansell crashes at the fast S-section behind the paddock at Suzuka after the Williams mounted a kerb during the Friday practice. It was the end of Mansell's Championship season.

Left Japan's Satoru Nakajima saved face for the home crowd by taking a point for sixth place in his Lotus. But Honda were embarrassed at not providing the winning engine on their own circuit.

tunnel. The 1987 Grand Prix took place a quarter of a century, almost to the day, since it was first opened.

The race attracted tremendous interest. Ticket sales were so heavily oversubscribed that would-be spectators had to ballot to decide who could buy them. Naturally, the Honda hierarchy were there in force, confidently expecting their so-successful engines to produce yet another victory.

They were to be disappointed, not only in the race but also in qualifying: for the first time in 1987 there was no Honda-powered car on the front row. Pole went to Berger's Ferrari and Prost was alongside in his McLaren; on row two were Boutsen (Benetton) and Alboreto in the other Ferrari. Piquet only fifth fastest qualifier, was in row three. With Senna's Lotus-Honda on the fourth row and Satoru Nakajima on row six in the other Lotus (despite his intimate knowledge of the track) there were already glum faces in the Honda camp.

Berger quickly demonstrated that his pole effort was no fluke. He streaked into the lead at once and, apart from one lap when he changed tyres, held it right to the finish. At last Ferrari had fulfilled the promise shown in recent races, and Berger's victory, only his second, was the first time one of the red cars had won since the German GP in 1985, 27 months earlier.

Victory was made easier for Berger when Prost, who had been quickest in the pre-race warm-up, suffered a puncture on lap two and lost a couple of laps as he crawled back to his pit for a fresh tyre. The way Prost drove after that, slicing through the field from last place, setting the lap record and finishing seventh, suggested he would have given Berger tough opposition but for that flat.

Hopes of a Ferrari one-two were dashed at the start when Alboreto, with clutch trouble, stalled on the line and set off from the back of the field. By the end he had hauled himself up to finish a

Above *Brazilian Roberto Moreno forced his sluggish AGS into 27th (reserve) qualifying place. He made his first-ever F1 start as a result of Mansell's withdrawal.*

1 Gerhard Berger (Ferrari F1/87)	1h 32m 58.072s, 119.829mph	
2 Ayrton Senna (Lotus-Honda 99T)	1h 33m 15.456s	
3 Stefan Johansson (MacLaren-TAG MP4/3)	1h 33m 15.766s	
4 Michele Alboreto (Ferrari F1/87)	1h 34m 18.513s	
5 Thierry Boutsen (Benetton-Ford B187)	1h 34m 23.648s	
6 Satoru Nakajima (Lotus-Honda 99T)	1h 34m 34.551s	

Fastest lap *Alain Prost (McLaren-TAG MP4/3), 1m 43.844s, 126.210mph*

useful fourth. The prancing horse was back in business!

After Prost's early problem Boutsen took his Benetton into second place; but Berger extended his lead and after a 10-lap chase the Belgian had to ease back with an inactive clutch and too-high fuel consumption. He eventually finished a disappointed fifth.

After 12 laps Senna was second and Piquet third. If anything had happened to the up-front Ferrari, Honda's face would have been saved. But Berger never put a foot wrong and his car stayed healthy.

Following the flurry of mid-race tyre changes, Johansson lay second in his McLaren. Perhaps a Honda-engined car would make no higher than third at the finish? But Johansson was running into a problem; his TAG engine was proving too thirsty, and as he cut back his turbo boost Senna closed on him. Trying desperately to

conserve fuel and still stay ahead of the Lotus, Johansson's hopes were dashed when Senna passed him coming out of the final corner!

New world champion Piquet, who needed no further points but was under pressure to do well for Honda (who were paying his very considerable fee), did make something of an effort. For lap after lap after half the distance he tagged Senna and once almost got by when Senna missed a gear. But the effort ended miserably when his engine overheated, probably the result of picking up debris in a radiator, and expired in a cloud of smoke with only five laps to go.

To the delight of the crowd, Nakajima managed to scrape into sixth place when Cheever's Arrows ran short of petrol just before the finish. Another champion was crowned in Japan. Jonathan Palmer finished his Tyrrell eighth overall but first of the non-turbo cars to make sure of the Jim Clark Cup.

Below *Gerhard Berger won in tremendous style – afterwards thanking Mansell for helping him learn the tight circuit by driving him round in a road car before the practice sessions.*

BERGER DOMINATES DOWN-UNDER

For Mansell, Read 'Patrese'

Winning a race provides an added momentum, for both driver and team, and Gerhard Berger went to Adelaide confident that he and Ferrari could do the trick again. The Austrian was hardly in top physical shape, suffering from a virus infection and earache, but that did not prevent him from grabbing his second pole in succession, producing fastest time in the pre-race warm-up, and leading the race on every lap to add to his Japanese triumph.

When he had signed for Ferrari for 1987, there were those who suggested he had switched too early and would have done better to stay another maturing season with Benetton. These last two races had proved that Enzo Ferrari had been right in signing him and that Berger had been shrewd in taking up the Commendatore's offer.

Although the drivers' championship had been decided, and Williams had lapped everyone for the constructors' title, Adelaide produced fine weather, slick organisation and an entertaining race. With rule changes due for 1988 this grand prix marked the end of 4-bar turbo-boost (to be cut to 2.5 bar) and the 195-litre tankage for turbos (to be trimmed to 150). It was the swansong of the Porsche-built TAG engine which had done McLaren proud for four seasons. It was the last time out for a Williams with Honda power. And it was the first grand prix for Stefano Modena, European Formula 3000 champion, whose debut gave promise of a future F1 star. Modena had been drafted by Brabham to replace Riccardo Patrese, who had been given early release to substitute for the injured Mansell before becoming a Williams regular in 1988.

Once again, as in Japan, Prost was with Berger on the front of the grid. But Adelaide, which had brought Prost his second successive championship a year earlier, was not to smile upon him again; he was third for most of the first half of the race, then second for a few laps, but later succumbed to a brake problem — which also brought retirement for team-mate Johansson, having his last McLaren drive.

While no-one could make any real impact on the flying Berger, there was a tight battle behind for almost half the race, with Piquet heading Prost, Alboreto and Senna in close formation. Piquet dropped out of contention when he had

Below Ayrton Senna drove hard to take second spot in his last outing for Lotus – but was then disqualified for having oversized brake ducting.

Right Formula 3000 champion Stefano Modena made his F1 debut at Adelaide in a Brabham, holding 12th place before retiring on lap 32.

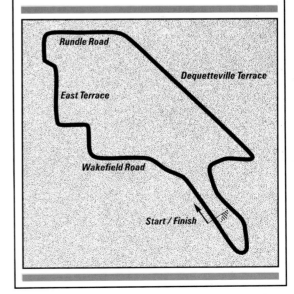

AUSTRALIAN GRAND PRIX
— 15 November —

82 laps, 192.5 miles

Adelaide fought off opposition from other cities to stage Australia's first F1 GP in 1985. Uses public roads and part of the race-horse course. Very well organised.

Rundle Road

Dequetteville Terrace

East Terrace

Wakefield Road

Start / Finish

to stop for fresh tyres, and Senna took up the pursuit of Berger at half distance. It was a gritty effort by Senna in his last outing for Lotus before switching to McLaren, and he raised Lotus hopes by steadily cutting back Berger's lead.

With 20 laps to go Senna was less than nine seconds behind, but then began to drift back as his tyres lost their edge and Berger crammed on more pressure. With 10 laps to go Berger demonstrated his dominance by setting a new lap record, and came home an impressive winner.

All Senna's effort later went for nought. There was a protest that the brake-cooling ducts on his car were wider than permitted, and he was excluded from the results. So Alboreto, who had finished third, was upgraded to second place and Ferrari got their first one-two since Alboreto and Johansson had done the trick in the 1985 Canadian GP. Senna's exclusion elevated Boutsen to third, his best placing all season.

Neither Williams managed to finish. Like several other drives, Piquet found his brakes fading and then retired with a loose gearshift, while Patrese's drive ended with engine failure. Although the Williams team had comfortably taken the constructors' title for the second year running (and the fourth time in all) they had just failed to beat McLaren's record 143½ points scored in 1984.

Palmer had a banging match with Warwick on only the second lap, which might have brought retirement. He had to pit for a new tyre and struggled throughout with his Tyrrell's front suspension bent, which hardly made for confident handling. But with Streiff spinning off early, Alliot the victim of electrical gremlins, and Capelli another retirement, Palmer came in fifth, to be placed fourth after Senna's exclusion, for the best finish of his GP career, and quite a feat for a non-turbo entry. In only his third grand prix, Frenchman Yannick Dalmas placed fifth in a Lola while Brazilian Roberto Moreno, in his second GP outing came sixth in an AGS.

The Williams team, which had won nine of the season's 16 GPs (six to Mansell and three to Piquet) had failed to pick up any points in the final two rounds. Prost finished the series with three wins for McLaren, Senna with two for Lotus, and Berger the final two for Ferrari. The Benetton team had often looked challenging but

Below *Gerhard Berger felt unwell at Adelaide – but he dominated practice, took pole position, and led for all but the first few hundred yards of the race. Ferrari had left it pretty late. But they finished the season in high fettle, and most fans were glad to see them back in the frame.*

were often beset with niggling problems, while Brabham were but a shadow of their former selves.

The season ended on a high note for Ferrari, which was good not only for Berger but also for the sport; for without the red cars on the grid and doing well, motor racing lacks something of its charisma. The Japanese and Australian GPs served notice that the Italian team was firmly back in business and would offer a real threat to the opposition in the coming season.

Above *Frenchman Yannick Dalmas (Lola), second fastest of the non-turbo contenders at Adelaide, finished fifth; but he scored no points because his car had not participated in the full championship round.*

1 Gerhard Berger (Ferrari F1/87)		1h 52m 56.144s, 102.229mph
2 Michele Alboreto (Ferrari F1/87)		1h 54m 04.028s
3 Thierry Boutsen (Benetton-Ford B187)		1 lap down
4 Jonathan Palmer (Tyrrell-Cosworth DG/016)		2 laps down
5 Yannick Dalmas (Lola-Cosworth LC87)		3 laps down
6 Roberto Moreno (AGS-Cosworth JH22)		3 laps down
Fastest lap *Berger, 1m 20.416s, 105.123mph*		

INDEX

Italic figures refer to the captions

Acknowledgements

The publishers thank the following organisations and individuals for permission to reproduce the photographs in this book:

Action-Plus 133, 152–3, 154, 168, 183, 186–7; AllSport/Chris Cole 153; AllSport/Vandystadt 73 inset, 75, 80, 103, 108–9, 116–7, 123 inset, 139, 140, 148–9, 156–7, 161 below, 165, 180; Charles Briscoe-Knight 52–3, 58, 61, 64–5, 67, 85, 87, 92–3, 102–3, 111, 119, 122–3, 124–5, 128–9, 134, 136, 138–9, 143, 144, (Colin Baker) 150–1, 151, 169, 171 top, 172–3; Diana Burnett 63, 84, 89, 105 inset, 106, 127 top; Colorsport 178; Colorsport/SIPA (Amaduzzi) 179, (Brocard) 110–1, (Compoint) 2–3, 4–5, 50–1, 53, 74–5, 76 top, 78, 79, 104–5, 120–1, 130, 131, 140–1, 147, 184–5, 187, (Curtet) 69, (De Nombel) 1, 68, 72–3, 162–3, 164–5, 174–5, (Giacomini) 132–3, (Kith) 182–3, (Marguerat) 166–7, 175, (Morvan) 96–7, (Taillade) 114, 136–7, 146–7, 155, 157, 158, 160–1, (Taylor) 142–3, 145; Mirco Decet 15 above; DPPI 41, (Gilles/Levent) 56–7, 94–5, (Levent/Vargioulu) 54–5, 62–3, 68, 86–7; Geoffrey Goddard 12 below, 13, 14, 15 below, 18, 21 above, 22, 32, 33, 34–5, 38–9, 46, 47 above; Dave Kennard 90–1, 98–9; LAT Photographic 6, 20 below, 30 below, 36–7, 39, 40, 41, 43, 44, 45, 48–9; Popperfoto 27, 30 above, 31, 35; Cyril Posthumus 17 below, 20 above; RAC 10–11; Peter Roberts Collection/Neill Bruce 8–9, 11, 12 above, 14 inset, 16, 17 above, 22–3, 28–9; Nigel Snowdon 42–3, 56, 60, 107, 135, 159, 162, 170–1, 173, 176–7, 180–1, 184, 188, 189; Sporting Pictures 58–9, 81, 82, 100, 100–1, 115, 118–9; Sutton Photographic 66, 88, 112–3, 120 inset.
Ian Dawson (Octopus Publishing Group Picture Library) 18–9, 24, 26–7.

JACKET PICTURES Front cover Nigel Mansell (Colorsport/SIPA). Back cover Gerhard Berger (Charles Briscoe-Knight); Alessandro Nannini (Action-Plus); Alain Prost (Colorsport/SIPA); Nelson Piquet (AllSport)